MEASUREMENT AND EVALUATION
OF HEALTH EDUCATION

With Contributions on Qualitative Evaluation
By

Allan B. Steckler, DR.P.H.

Professor and Associate Dean
Department of Health Behavior and Health Education
School of Public Health
University of North Carolina at Chapel Hill
Chapel Hill, North Carolina

and

Robert M. Goodman, PH.D., M.P.H.

Associate Professor
Department of Health Promotion and Education
School of Public Health
University of South Carolina
Columbia, South Carolina

MEASUREMENT AND EVALUATION OF HEALTH EDUCATION

Third Edition

By

MARK B. DIGNAN, PH.D., M.P.H.

Associate Professor
Department of Family and Community Medicine
Bowman Gray School of Medicine of
Wake Forest University
Winston-Salem, North Carolina

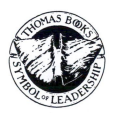

CHARLES C THOMAS • PUBLISHER
Springfield • Illinois • U.S.A.

Published and Distributed Throughout the World by

CHARLES C THOMAS • PUBLISHER
2600 South First Street
Springfield, Illinois 62794-9265

© *1995 by* CHARLES C THOMAS • PUBLISHER
ISBN 0-398-05935-7 (cloth)
ISBN 0-398-05958-6 (paper)
Library of Congress Catalog Card Number: 94-30631

First Edition, 1986
Second Edition, 1989
Third Edition, 1995

Printed in the United States of America
SC-R-3

Library of Congress Cataloging-in-Publication Data

Dignan, Mark B.
    Measurement and evaluation of health education / by Mark B. Dignan
; with contributions on qualitative evaluation by Allan B. Steckler
and Robert M. Goodman. — 3rd ed.
        p.   cm.
    Includes bibliographical references and index.
    ISBN 0-398-05935-7. — ISBN 0-398-05958-6 (pbk.)
    1. Health education—Evaluation. 2. Health education—Evaluation
—Statistical methods. I. Steckler, Allan B. II. Goodman, Robert
M. III. Title.
RA440.4.D53   1995
610'.28'7—dc20
                                                                94-30631
                                                                CIP

For Kay

PREFACE

This book is intended as a text for those interested in the evaluation of health education and health promotion programs. In addition to students, this text is also intended for health professionals and others who find themselves needing to know about program evaluation but whose training did not include the subject. The text does not presume that readers have an extensive background, but an appreciation of the concepts underlying health education and health promotion and a basic awareness of statistics will prove helpful. Neither is a prerequisite to understanding, however.

This is the third edition of *MEASUREMENT AND EVALUATION OF HEALTH EDUCATION.* As in previous editions, this text is based on the notion that measurement and evaluation are linked: measurement is one of the fundamental tools needed for evaluation, and evaluation design provides the direction needed to use measurement effectively. The text is organized into two main sections. The first section focuses on measurement and includes chapters on measurement theory, accuracy, and applications to measurement of knowledge, attitudes and behaviors. The second section presents the principles of evaluation and includes chapters on evaluation design, data analysis and presentation of results. Several notable changes from previous editions have been introduced in this third edition of the text, most notably greater emphasis on evaluation of health education programs conducted in community settings. An emphasis on evaluation of programs for the community, as opposed to those for clinical populations or schools, is important because community programs bring with them much of the uncertainty and complexity faced by those conducting evaluations. Discussion of the complexity and uncertainty in evaluation is critical to developing an understanding of program evaluation. In addition to the emphasis on community health education programs, description and discussion of measurement instruments has been expanded in the third edition, and presentation of validity and reliability has been broadened. Finally, the treatment of the qualitative approach to evaluation that was provided so well by Allan Steckler and Bob Goodman in the second edition has been retained.

Since publication of the second edition of *MEASUREMENT AND EVALUATION OF HEALTH EDUCATION,* I have been privileged to share my work in program evaluation with a superb group of professional colleagues and students. I am indebted to these fine people for continually challenging me to examine and update my ideas on measurement and evaluation. I owe a special debt of gratitude to another group: those I have encountered in managing community health education projects. These people have continually amazed me with their creativity and insight into the challenges of conducting evaluations in community settings. Through our interactions, these people have reinforced one of the most lasting lessons from my upbringing: people should be judged on their merits as people and not by their level of academic training. Community health education depends heavily on such people, and I feel very lucky to have had their company from time to time.

Preparation of this edition of *MEASUREMENT AND EVALUATION OF HEALTH EDUCATION* was aided by the considerable talents of several key individuals. Carol Hill Thomas provided valuable editorial assistance, and her diligence and patience is appreciated. Allan Steckler and Bob Goodman contributed much of the content and examples regarding qualitative evaluation in the second edition. Their willingness to allow continued use of their work in the third edition is also appreciated. Finally, this revision would not have been completed without the encouragement, patience and input from my wife, Kay.

M.B.D.

CONTENTS

MEASUREMENT AND EVALUATION OF HEALTH EDUCATION

Chapter 1

INTRODUCTION

Evaluation is the process of comparing observations with a standard. In this book, the observations we focus on are the activities and results associated with health education and health promotion. The standards we use in our evaluation are the expectations that we have for the programs.

Measurement is an integral part of evaluation. For our purposes in this book, we can define measurement as the process of assigning labels or values to observations. As you might guess, measurement of health education and health promotion programs is complicated. The complexity of measurement arises because we make choices in what to observe, in how to label our observations, and in what standards to use for comparison. For example, suppose we were to evaluate a weight management program for adults with diabetes. In collecting observations about the program, we could choose to focus on the participants' weights, assuming that effective management would be evident in how much the participants weighed. We could collect the participants' weights before, during and after the program and consider the change in weight as evidence of the program's effectiveness. Just as there were choices to be made with the observations, the standards that we use to compare with what we observe could also come from a variety of sources. One source of standards could be a table of ideal body weights used to reference each individual's weight. If the ideal body weight table is used as the standard, the program results would be interpreted in terms of how the participants' weights moved toward the ideal body weight during the program.

An alternative approach to the evaluation of a weight management program for diabetes might include an assessment of the participants' knowledge of meal planning. Measuring the participants' knowledge of how to plan meals might seem like a good idea because it would give us information about a change occurring within the individual (ability to plan meals) as a result of the program that could be used in controlling diabetes, as well as in managing weight. We could derive the standards

3

for evaluating meal planning skills based on measurements collected at the beginning of the program. These measurements would then serve as a "baseline" standard for comparing measurements carried out during and after the program. If the program is effective, the participants' meal planning skills would improve as shown by measurements made during and after the program.

Evaluating the weight management program in terms of body weight would provide evidence of the overall effectiveness of the program, but would not tell us very much about whether the participants learned how to keep the weight off without help from the program. Focusing on meal planning, on the other hand, would give information about weight management skills but would not tell us whether the skills could be used effectively. Figure 1-1 illustrates our dilemma.

Evaluation Option A

The participant's weight is the most important outcome for the program. The program will only be successful if a participant can get closer to his/her ideal weight.

Program Objectives

Adults with diabetes need to learn to manage their weight. This program will manage their diet, thereby helping them get closer to their ideal weight. Participants will also learn how to plan their meals, which will build their skills and enable them to manage their weight on their own.

Which option to Choose, A, B or Both ?

Evaluation Option B

Getting closer to their ideal weight is not the most important outcome for the program. If the participant has not learned how to manage his/her weight, they will soon be right back to the unhealthy weight where they were before they participated in the program.

Figure 1-1. The statement on the left summarizes the objectives of the weight management program. Two options for program evaluation are shown on the right as Evaluation Options A and B.

Why not measure body weight and meal planning skills? If we weighed the participants and measured their meal planning skills as well, then we could combine the information from the two measures and make statements about the association between progress in weight control and meal planning ability. Combining the information collected from the two types of measurements increases the usefulness of the evaluation because it allows us to see how the instruction on meal planning interacts with the ultimate goals of the program. We anticipate that the interaction will be positive and productive and that those who learn how to plan their meals will be able to control their weight. We should be open-minded, however, and willing to accept information that suggests only a weak relationship between meal planning and weight control, or even a negative relationship. (A negative relationship would be one where those with better meal planning cannot control their weight.)

Program Evaluation

A program is a series of activities that are developed to achieve specific objectives. Program evaluation is the application of the principles of evaluation for the purpose of learning about the program and its progress toward achieving its objectives. In summary, program evaluation includes clarifying questions about a program and its effects, collecting data about the program, and analyzing the data to develop conclusions about the program in question. Evaluation should be carried out in a systematic fashion. Figure 1-2 shows steps for carrying out evaluation systematically. In discussing the six steps, we'll introduce many of the topics that will be covered throughout the book.

1. **Objectives:**   Define what the evaluation is expected to accomplish
2. **Mechanism:**   Describes how results are to be produced by the program
3. **Definitions:**   Specify characteristics of the program and its outcomes
4. **Evaluation design:** Outlines process of collecting information
5. **Analysis:**   Describes how information collected for evaluation will be used
6. **Report of results:** Compares observations with objectives and draws conclusions

Figure 1-2. Six Steps in carrying out evaluation

Once the need for evaluation is determined, the first step is to establish objectives to guide the evaluation. The objectives spell out what is expected from the evaluation; what should be accomplished, in other words. Using the objectives of the program as a guide, the second step is to decide on a mechanism for the processes that produce the outcomes that are to be evaluated. The third step is to develop key definitions needed to structure the evaluation. The definitions should specify the information that will be needed for the evaluation, the standard to be used for comparison and how comparisons will be made, and the objects and methods for any measurement needed. Using the objectives, mechanism and definitions as a basis, the fourth step is to develop a design for measurement and collection of information needed for the evaluation (commonly called "data collection"). The fifth step in developing the evaluation is to plan for analyzing the information that is collected. Analysis includes the procedures that will be needed to guide the development of conclusions from the information collected in the evaluation. The sixth and final step in evaluation is reporting results. Reporting can take a number of forms, depending on the circumstances, but in any case the report must be developed carefully, with the objectives for the evaluation clearly in mind. Regardless of the reason, evaluation should include the same basic components. In the next section, we will present an example that illustrates many of the principles and decisions that are involved with developing and carrying out evaluation.

Evaluation of Community Health Education about Cancer

The American Cancer Society has long promoted the notion that the best way to prevent death from cancer is through early detection. It is true that for most cancers, the earlier the disease is detected, the more favorable the outcome. For this reason, there have been many different public health education campaigns carried out in the past decades focusing on increasing screening for cancer. Among the most well known of these campaigns have been those focusing on breast and cervical cancer. These two cancers are among the most common causes of cancer death among women. The public education campaigns about breast and cervical cancer have promoted the idea that these cancers can be attacked by early detection. Breast Self Examination (BSE), breast examinations by health care providers, and mammograms have been advocated as techniques for finding breast cancer, and the Pap smear has been widely recognized as a test that can find cervical cancer in its early stages of development.

In this example, we will discuss the evaluation of a community health education program for breast and cervical cancer. These two cancers were selected because they were of great importance to the community and because there are screening tests for them that are effective. The entire community was the target population for this program, which advocated that women see their doctor regularly and obtain Pap smears, breast exams and, if indicated, mammograms. Women were also encouraged to examine their breasts regularly, and instruction was provided. To ensure that the program reached the women, two types of methods were used. Mass media was used to reach the community as a whole, using television, radio and newspapers. For women known to be at high risk of breast cancer, those with a family history, for example, intensive individual and group instruction was made available.

Evaluation of the program was to focus on the entire community and was to be carried out by comparing women that received the educational program with similar women who did not receive the program. A similar community was selected to supply women who would not receive the program. (This community would receive the educational program after the evaluation was completed, however.) The steps shown in Figure 1-2 will guide us through discussion of how the evaluation was carried out.

For **Step one** shown in Figure 1-2, the principal objective of the cancer prevention program was to address the problem of cancer among women in the community by increasing Pap smears, breast exams and mammograms among women in the community. Stated more formally, the objectives were to: (1) increase the percentage of women in the community age 18 and older who receive annual Pap smears and breast exams and (2) increase the percentage of women, age 50 and older, who receive annual mammograms.

Step two of Figure 1-2 suggests that evaluation is helped when there is a mechanism that explains how the program's results are to be produced. Health education is based on the central concept that clear communication of the idea that taking action to protect your health is worth the cost, and it is likely to result in better health in the long run. For the cancer prevention program, the essential features of a mechanism explaining how the program would result in more women in the community obtaining Pap smears, breast exams and mammograms is depicted in the three steps shown in Figure 1-3.

The three-step mechanism shown in Figure 1-3 provides a simple but important structure for the evaluation. The mechanism shows that women must be exposed to the program messages in order for change to occur. This means that the evaluation must be designed to detect whether

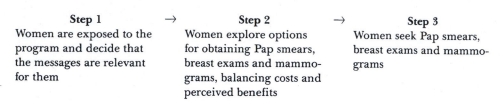

Step 1	→	**Step 2**	→	**Step 3**
Women are exposed to the program and decide that the messages are relevant for them		Women explore options for obtaining Pap smears, breast exams and mammograms, balancing costs and perceived benefits		Women seek Pap smears, breast exams and mammograms

Figure 1-3. A mechanism explaining how public health education can influence women to obtaining cancer screening

women in the community become aware of the messages as a separate issue from whether they obtain cancer screening or not. In addition, the mechanism implies that the evaluation will have to be structured to detect changes that occur **after** the program messages are introduced to the community, and to identify changes that could have occurred because of other occurrences in the community that were not part of the program.

The **third step** shown in Figure 1-2 refers to definitions that are needed to structure evaluation. Having thought through a basic mechanism that describes how the program would function (see Figure 1-3) points out the need for clear definitions for the program, its targets and results. Based on this realization, the following definitions were developed.

> *Cancer prevention program:* The program designed to be implemented in the community. The program includes two principal components: mass media and direct education. Mass media includes television and radio public service announcements and printed materials such as posters, brochures and flyers. Direct education will be carried out through presentations that can be used with social and civic groups in the community, as well as in waiting rooms of the local health care providers.
>
> *Target population:* The program will focus on women who are residents of the community and who are not planning on moving away from the community before the evaluation is completed. Women, age 18 and older, are the primary targets for breast and cervical cancer prevention. Women age 50 and older are the primary targets for breast cancer detection with mammography.
>
> *Program Results:* The primary results from the program will be the responses from the women in the target population to survey items about their most recent Pap smear, breast exam and mammogram. The mammogram information must be collected with the age of the woman clearly in mind, since mammography is not recommended

as a routine practice for women under age 50. Secondary program results will be records describing the activities of the educational program. These records will include the dates and times that the television and radio public service announcements were broadcast, and similar information on distribution of printed cervical cancer education materials. Records of the direct education component of the program will include the dates of presentations, attendance and a summary of questions asked by the audience.

Step four in Figure 1-2 addresses the evaluation design. An evaluation design is a plan for collecting information needed to answer questions about the program. For the cancer prevention program, the design for evaluation would be a "before-and-after" approach with a comparison community. The decision to use a comparison community for the evaluation was not made easily. Evaluation is expensive and collecting information in two communities would just about double the cost of evaluation. However, changes in women's knowledge, attitudes and behaviors regarding breast and cervical cancer may occur in the community whether the program functions well or not, particularly if public awareness of these diseases changes. For example, there have been several instances when famous women developed breast cancer, and their experiences were publicized widely. Such publicity may function just like a planned public health education program and influence women to seek screening. To account for such changes, in addition to overall changes in attitudes toward cancer, data from a comparison community was needed by the evaluation. The comparison community selected was quite similar to the community receiving the educational program in terms of the population and available health services, but did not receive the same television and radio stations. Information on cancer screening was obtained by telephone surveys carried out before and after the educational program was implemented. The evaluation design used is shown in Figure 1-4. The telephone survey was selected as the method for collecting evaluation information because of concerns with the ability to reach the target population and the cost of evaluation. The cost of conducting the surveys by telephone is much less than it would be for face-to-face interviews, and it was known that approximately 90% of households in both the program and comparison communities had telephones. To carry out the evaluation, randomly selected samples of 500 women were interviewed by telephone in the program and control communities before the program was implemented and again afterward. A consultant statistician assisted with selecting the sample sizes of 500. She calculated that with 500 women interviewed, the evaluation would have enough power to detect a change of 10 percentage points in the percent of women reporting that they had a Pap smear during the past year between the baseline and the post-program survey. The baseline and post-program surveys were carried out independently. That is, women had the same chance of being selected for the survey before and after the program.

	Time 1	Time 2	Time 3
Program Community	0	X	0
Comparison Community	0		0

O—Survey carried out
X—Educational program implemented

Figure 1-4. The evaluation design for the community cancer education program

The samples of women were selected by calling them at their homes. Telephone numbers were selected using a random-digit-dialing technique. The random-digit-dialing technique uses a computer to generate lists of telephone numbers at random. Blocks of telephone numbers that are known to be reserved for businesses and institutions such as universities, hospitals and government offices were eliminated from the list automatically to reduce the number of calls made to places other than households. Once the interviewer reached a household where women lived, the project and the interview were described and the evaluation information was collected.

Step five shown in Figure 1-2 brings up the topic of analysis of information collected for the evaluation. The goal of analysis is to answer the questions raised about the program. In some cases, analysis requires sophisticated statistics. In many instances, however, analysis merely requires reporting the data in an appropriate form. Regardless, analysis begins with review of the objectives of the program. In this case, the primary question to be answered by analysis was whether the percentage of women reporting that they obtained cancer screening (Pap smears, breast exams, mammograms) increased more in the community that received the program than in the comparison community. A second critical issue was whether women in the community were aware of the public education program. Answers to these questions are shown in Figure 1-5.

A. Numbers of women reporting that they had seen, heard or read about breast or cervical cancer prevention in the community during the past year.

	Baseline Survey	Post-Program Survey
Program Community	119	256
Comparison Community	110	133

B. Numbers of women reporting having a Pap smear during the past year.

	Baseline Survey	Post-Program Survey
Program Community	271	335
Comparison Community	285	273

C. Numbers of women, age 50 and older, reporting having a mammogram during the past year.

	Baseline Survey	Post-Program Survey
Program Community	53	70
Comparison Community	61	59

Figure 1-5. Telephone Survey Results for the program and comparison communities at baseline and after the program (post-program)

Using the data shown in Figure 1-5, the task of analysis was to decide whether the changes that occurred during the program were greater than would have been expected by chance alone. Statistical testing can be helpful in answering this question. (A thorough discussion of statistical testing is beyond the scope of this book, so we will treat this topic lightly. Additional readings on data analysis and statistics are suggested at the end of the chapter.) Our statistical consultant explained that an odds ratio would enable us to test whether the pattern of numbers in Figure 1-5 are different from what would be expected by chance alone. The logic is as follows: if the program had no effect, then the pattern of numbers should not be different from what we might get if we did a random telephone survey of the population. If the program was effective, however, the pattern of answers to the telephone survey should be affected in a systematic way. That is, more women should report having Pap smears and mammograms after the program than before and, in addition, more women should report that they saw, heard or read about the program. Our statistics consultant explained that the odds ratios indicated that more women knew about the program and that more women in the program community reported Pap smears at the post-program survey, but that there was no difference in the number of women reporting a mammogram in the program and comparison communities.

The **sixth step** in Figure 1-2 is the report from the evaluation. The key elements that make a difference between a successful and unsuccessful report is matching the level of detail with the audience. For all reports, however, the single most important elements are the statements that declare whether the program functioned as intended or fell short. Many readers will rapidly lose interest in evaluation reports once they have developed a sense of how the program functioned. They have relatively little interest in explanations about how or why the program may have functioned, and they are satisfied with simple answers to what they see as fundamental questions. Readers who are interested in learning how the conclusions about the program were derived require detailed descriptions of the processes involved with each step in the evaluation. For these readers, it would be necessary to include descriptions of the target populations studied, how women to provide evaluation information were selected, and the questionnaire used and how it was developed. The data collected would be described in considerable detail, providing enough information for the reader to come to their own conclusions about the program.

For our cancer education program, Figure 1-6 illustrates the results of the evaluation. These simple histograms show the differences in the data collected from the program and control communities at the baseline and post-program interviews. Histograms, pie charts and other graphic presentations that illustrate evaluation results are appreciated by most audiences, but particularly by those who are not technically oriented.

QUALITATIVE EVALUATION METHODS

In the community cancer prevention program example, we chose to report the number of women who reported hearing about the program, as well as those reporting that they obtained Pap smears and mammograms. When we describe the results of the project using numbers, we are **quantifying** our results. Quantitative measures provide answers to questions in numerical terms, but if you are concerned with **why** some women obtained screening and others did not, or how the cancer education program may have influenced women, the quantitative approach will not be satisfactory. A qualitative approach that is designed to provide descriptions and explanations is needed.

Qualitative evaluation applies methods used by anthropologists to study cultures, i.e., a group that shares the same rules and understandings. University students, military personnel, church parishioners, and even cancer patients can be considered members of cultural groups. Like

**A.   Frequency of women reporting that they were aware of cancer
prevention program materials in their community.   Telephone surveys
conducted in the program and comparison communities at baseline and
post-program.**

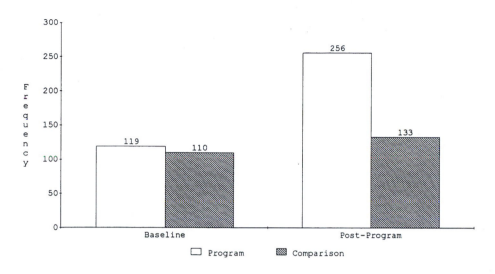

**B.   Frequency of women reporting having a Pap smear within the past
year.   Telephone surveys conducted in the program and comparison
communities at baseline and post-program.**

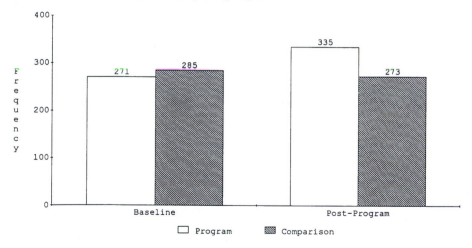

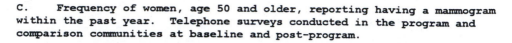

C.   Frequency of women, age 50 and older, reporting having a mammogram
within the past year.   Telephone surveys conducted in the program and
comparison communities at baseline and post-program.

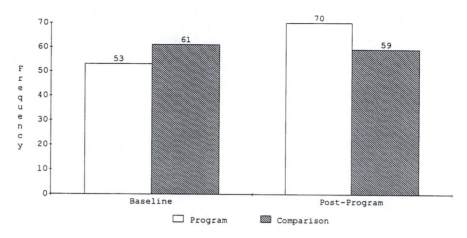

Figure 1-6. Histograms illustrating the results from the telephone surveys conducted before and after the program in the program and comparison communities. Part A shows results from questions about awareness of the program, part B reports frequency of Pap smears, and part C reports frequency of mammograms.

anthropologists, health professionals can study such groups by immersing themselves in the culture and observing, participating, interviewing key people, doing case studies, and analyzing existing written documents. The goal in using such qualitative methods is to get an "insider's" view of the group under study, to understand how and why its members perceive and interpret things the way they do. By getting such an insider's view, anthropologists learn about different cultures and are then able to develop theories which explain cultures around the world.

The reason for using qualitative methods in evaluation of health education and health promotion programs is to get an insider's view of a program and to understand why and how the program worked or did not work. The qualitative evaluator is like an anthropologist, but instead of studying an exotic culture, the evaluator applies the anthropologist's methods to examine a program and its impact. Such information helps the evaluator understand how people perceive a program, why people reacted to it the way they did, and why it had the effect it did. By understanding why and how programs work or do not work, health professionals are better able to improve their future programs. The specific methods for carrying out this process are further discussed in Chapters 8, 9 and 10.

Qualitative methods are often compared with quantitative methods. Quantitative methods use experimental or quasi-experimental designs in which comparisons are made between treated and untreated subjects or groups. (Quasi-experimental designs include many of the elements of ordinary experiments, but cannot achieve the degree of control possible in the laboratory.) Quantitative methods tend to focus on program impact and outcomes that are measurable in the strict sense of the word, i.e., what the results of the program were. Quantitative methods most often address the question of what specific effects the program "caused," i.e., what changes in knowledge, attitudes and behaviors occurred as a result of the health education program.

Quantitative evaluation has been criticized for limiting attention to measurable program effects and ignoring the processes thought to produce effects. The lack of information collected by quantitative evaluation about the processes that produced the effects make it very difficult to learn how and why a program succeeded or failed. Qualitative methods are useful in describing the elements or steps of a program, how the program was perceived by program targets, staff and others. Such documentation of perceptions is important for two reasons. First, it helps explain why the program produced the effects (impacts and outcomes) that it did, and second, it helps health educators develop a "theory" of interventions. By this we mean that the field of health education needs to build understanding of what programs (interventions) work and how they work in what settings and with what target populations. If we know only the results of health education programs and not how those effects were brought about, we cannot develop a body of knowledge which guides health educators in selecting the appropriate intervention for a particular target audience with a particular health problem, in a particular setting.

Using Quantitative and Qualitative Methods Together

Because of the need for evaluations to address both effects and processes, good evaluations should use both qualitative and quantitative approaches. The limitations of each approach are compensated for by the strengths of the other. Through qualitative methods, the context and functioning of a particular program can be described so that any results identified through quantitative methods can be understood and replicated.

EVALUATION AND HEALTH EDUCATION

Health education is just what it says: education focused on health. As education, the principles that underlie learning are very important to health education; but, because this type of education deals specifically with health and human behavior, the specific nature of diseases, their treatment, and especially their prevention, health education is distinct from many other forms of education. In addition, health education is directed toward every conceivable type of target population, from people seen for one-on-one diet counseling to viewers of mass media appeals for seat belt use.

Health education, like many other types of education, is usually focused on one or more of three targets: knowledge, attitudes, and/or behavior. Knowledge is perhaps the most intuitive target and has wide appeal. Most of us like to think that people can learn "the facts" and apply them properly. Casual conversation with people who are overweight will convince you that this idea is an oversimplification and that knowing how to control weight doesn't necessarily lead to controlled weight. On the other hand, it is probably unreasonable to expect people to control their weight if they don't know something about how their body uses food.

Attitudes are much less straightforward than knowledge. Attitudes are essentially opinions, and they are usually more difficult to assess than knowledge. Behaviors and attitudes strongly influence one another, although we cannot always be sure which came first. What we do know is that we need to have understanding of attitudes if we are to do a good job of educating people about their health.

Behavior is the third target of health education, and changing is perhaps the real reason for education in the first place. It is clear that, in many cases, people's behaviors are related directly to what they know (knowledge) and what they think (attitudes). In many other cases, however, behavior doesn't seem to be at all related to knowledge or attitudes as we have measured them.

PLAN FOR THE BOOK

The remaining chapters in this book are organized into two broad sections. The first section includes chapters that are devoted to the basic measurement skills needed to conduct and understand any evaluation.

This information is then applied to the design of evaluation, collection and analysis of data, and presentation of results in the chapters in the second section.

READINGS

Green, L.W., and Kreuter, M.W.: *Health Promotion Planning: An Educational and Environmental Approach.* Mountain View, CA, Mayfield, 1991.

Green, L.W., and Lewis, F.M.: *Measurement and Evaluation in Health Education and Health Promotion.* Palo Alto, Mayfield, 1986.

Miles, M.B., and Huberman, A.M.: *Qualitative Data Analysis: A Sourcebook of New Methods.* Beverly Hills, Sage, 1984.

Ross, Helen S., and Mico, Paul R.: *Theory and Practice in Health Education.* Palo Alto, Mayfield, 1980.

Windsor, R.A., Baranowski, T., Clark, N., and Cutter, G.: *Evaluation of Health Promotion and Education Programs.* Palo Alto, Mayfield, 1984.

Kleinbaum, D.G., Kupper, L.L., and Morgenstern, H.: *Epidemiologic Research: Principles and Quantitative Methods.* Belmont, CA, Lifetime Learning Publications, 1982.

Sarvela, P.D., and McDermott, R.J.: *Health Education Evaluation and Measurement: A Practitioner's Perspective.* Madison, WI, Brown & Benchmark, 1993.

Phillips, P.S.: *Basic Statistics for Health Science Students.* New York, Freeman, 1978.

Lien, A.J.: *Measurement and Evaluation of Learning,* 3rd ed. Dubuque, IA, Wm. C. Brown, 1976.

Part One
MEASUREMENT:
THE BASIS FOR EVALUATION

Chapter Two

THE NATURE OF MEASUREMENT

Evaluation is based on measurement—measurement of what people do, think, and feel. Because it is so basic, we'll start this chapter with an introduction to measurement. We'll begin with perhaps the most basic question: What is measurement? Before we consider an answer to this question formally, let's begin by exploring some of the more commonsense ideas. What does it mean to measure something? We use the word measurement in a wide variety of ways, but at its most basic level, to measure something is to describe it in a meaningful way using symbols. It is natural to think of measurement in terms of numbers exclusively, but it's important to realize that we can also think of measurement in other ways. For example, the size of this page would probably be measured in inches (maybe expressed as square inches) in the United States. Using inches as units to convey an idea about size or area is clearly measurement in a numerical fashion, but we could also say that this page is bigger or smaller than another and we would still be using measurement but in a different (less precise) form.

Measurement can also be considered a form of communication. The process of measurement conveys standard descriptions of the things measured that can be used by anyone who understands the units that are used. For example, a table measuring 120 inches by 72 inches might be described as "large," or maybe "average" or "small" in size. Regardless of how we might label it, the area of the table is still 8640 square inches. Labels can vary from person to person, but the square-inch area is objective and observable. The idea that we use numbers as well as language to describe objects leads to the concept that measurement includes both objective and subjective components. Let's look at the subjective aspect of measurement first.

Subjective Measurement

Put yourself in this situation. You are standing beside the freeway where your car has just broken down. As the cars whiz past, you sense that some are traveling faster than others. Your judgment of their speed as they pass by is mostly subjective. It is based on your own perceptions and is governed by your own internal mechanisms for quantifying such things as speed. Maybe it is the sound the cars make, or the amount of wind disturbance that occurs after the cars pass. Such factors are intuitive and mysterious elements of the measurement process and, naturally, will vary with the individual. Because such measurement is subjective, it would be practically impossible for you to be able to say that one car was traveling at 60 miles per hour and another at 62 miles per hour based solely on your own perceptions. As it turns out, we use subjective assessments as sort of shorthand descriptions for events and objects that we measure informally in our everyday lives. We would not need to be able to make 2 mph distinctions in such a case. Faster and slower will usually suffice. Figure 2-1 shows another case of subject measurement. Do the horizontal lines appear to be of equal length?

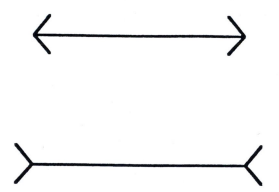

Figure 2-1. Judging the length of the lines by looking is an example of subjective measurement. The comparison between the two lines may vary from person to person.

Objective Measurement

The objective side of measurement is much more precise than the subjective. Objective measurement is necessary for us to accomplish many things that we do everyday. It is also subject to a much more rigorous set of rules than subjective measurement. As a general principle, objective measurement is usually preferred in situations where clear communication is needed and the costs of error are high, while subjective measurement is something that we use continuously and, for the most part, unconsciously. Adding objectivity can clarify measurement. As Figure 2-2 shows, the horizontal lines that we saw previously in Figure 2-1 are the same length.

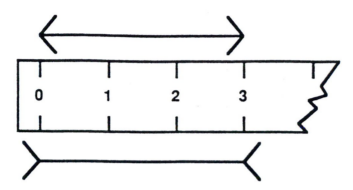

Figure 2-2. The ruler shows that the two lines are the same length. This is an example of **Objective Measurement**.

As a final thought, we also need to understand that measurement is really an abstract process. Recall the earlier example of the table. The use of inches or centimeters or any other unit that we may use to symbolize length is really an arbitrary definition created by humans for convenience and ease of communication. Because of this habit of using arbitrary units, we have many different systems of measurement currently in use around the world. All of the different systems are trying to accomplish one goal, however, and that is to assign symbols conveying units of value according to some set of rules. Remember, the units are arbitrary; the only reason they were developed was to help with communication.

SCALES OF MEASUREMENT

Units of measurement may seem arbitrary, but the systems of measurement that apply to different situations are not. As we tackle various measurement problems, we are actually using one of four basic approaches to assigning values to the things we measure. Sometimes the approaches overlap, but for the most part they are very different. The four approaches, "scales of measurement," are called nominal, ordinal, interval, and ratio. Let's examine these four categories in detail.

Nominal Scale Measurement

Nominal scale measurement attaches a label to that which is measured. Merely attaching labels may not seem like measurement, but the idea of assigning a name to symbolize something does make sense, in that the name distinguishes one thing from another. Let's consider an example. Male and female are names that we use to identify the sexes. The names are important distinctions and are used by our society to symbolize all the characteristics that we ascribe to maleness or femaleness. When we assign the label of male or female we are assigning a label to an individual according to a rule, which conforms to the basic definition of measurement that we put forth earlier. It is important to remember that nominal scale measurement doesn't convey any value to that which is measured but simply identifies or names it.

Ordinal Scale Measurement

Ordinal scale measurement assigns ranks to groups of objects of measurement. There is no specified difference between ranks, and the distinction between ranks is not necessarily equal; in fact, it is completely arbitrary. At the nominal level we simply named things. With the ordinal scale we not only name but our names imply a distinction of greater-than or less-than. Remember, despite the ordering there is no implication of distance between ranks. When we see someone and say she or he is tall, taller, or tallest, we are using our own rules to assign ranks (the names signify the rank). We rank people in terms of their height by comparing them with other people. Our rankings may be different from others, because they are based on our own ideas of height which may or may not be similar to others'.

Interval Scale Measurement

The third scale of measurement is called interval, but the name is somewhat of a misnomer. What is really meant by the term interval is equal interval. When we use interval scale measurement there is considerable advancement beyond the nominal and ordinal scales. Interval scale measurement assigns values to things according to predetermined rules. The intervals between values are of equal length, too. Because we have a system of intervals, it is impossible to have a value of zero, although virtually any other value is possible. This probably seems like a strange concept. Let's try to shed some light on this topic by looking at an example involving people's heights.

Using inches as our units, imagine two people whose heights are 60 and 64 inches. One is five feet even and the other is five feet four inches. Now imagine two more people whose heights are 72 and 76 inches, or 6 feet even and 6 feet four inches. The two sets of people are clearly different in height, but the difference between each one of the two pairs is the same distance of four inches. In other words, the interval scale that we use to measure height (inches) is such that the distance between each value on the scale is the same. Instead of having the ranks that we had with the ordinal scale where we called people tall and so on, we have numbers that are not based on arbitrary rules but on a predetermined system of assigning numeric values. Interval scale values have nearly all the properties of ordinary numbers. They can be added, subtracted, multiplied and divided, and the result has meaning. We could do arithmetic operations on nominal or ordinal scale values, of course, but the result would be impossible to interpret. For example, if we were to question 100 people about which hand was dominant and assigned the value of 1 to left-handedness and 2 to right-handedness, we could do any sort of mathematical procedure on the numbers that we wished. But the numbers are still nominal scale, and we wouldn't be able to interpret the results of our mathematical operations. What would an average-handedness value of 1.25 mean, for example, if the values of 1 and 2 mean left- and right-handedness? Many arithmetic operations don't make any sense with nominal and ordinal scale measures. With interval scale values, though, we DO have the ability to do arithmetic operations and get interpretable results. Remember the point about how interval scale measures don't include zero? This may seem strange, but can you imagine anyone of zero height? The scales of measurement that we use to measure many things such as height could conceivably include a value of zero, but it wouldn't make any sense.

Ratio Scale Measurement

Ratio scale measurements include zero, in addition to all the properties of interval scale measures. The intervals are of equal length and it makes sense to perform mathematical operations on the values. Most applications of ratio scales occur in the natural sciences; relatively few occur in social or behavioral science. For all practical purposes, though, ratio and interval scale measures are interchangeable.

To illustrate how scales of measurement come into play in evaluation, recall the example used in Chapter 1 describing the evaluation of the community-based breast and cervical cancer prevention program. In evaluating the effectiveness of the program, several different types of measurement could be used. For nominal scale measurement, evaluation would be limited to descriptions, such as listing the number of women answering yes to an item on the survey. Ordinal scale measurement could be obtained by ranking program participants in some way. Interval scale measurement requires use of an equal interval scale. Characteristics of women, such as their age or the number of years since their last Pap smear, could be used in interval scale measurement. Finally, evaluation could use ratio scale measurement by focusing on measures for which a value of zero has meaning. The difference in the number of women answering yes to certain survey items between "before" and "after" could legitimately be zero, thus qualifying the difference as a ratio scale measurement.

Nominal — Count the number of women who reported that they obtained Pap smears within the past year. *"78 out of the 120 women reported that they had a Pap smear within the past year."*

Ordinal — Arrange the women who reported that they obtained Pap smears within the past year by age groups. *"27% of women ages 18–29, 38% of women ages 30–44, 23% of women ages 45–64 and 11% of women age 65 and older reported Pap smears."* Figure 2-3 illustrates how the distribution of women reporting a Pap smear within the past year by age group might look.

Interval — Compute the average age of women reporting that they obtained a Pap smear within the past year. *"The average age of women who reported that they had a Pap smear within the past year was 40.8. The average age of women who did NOT report a Pap smear within the past year was 43.4."*

Ratio — Compute the difference in the number of women reporting that they had obtained a Pap smear within the past year between the baseline and post-program suveys. *"The difference in the average age of women who did and did not report having a Pap smear in the past year was 2.6 years." (This number could conceivably be zero.)*

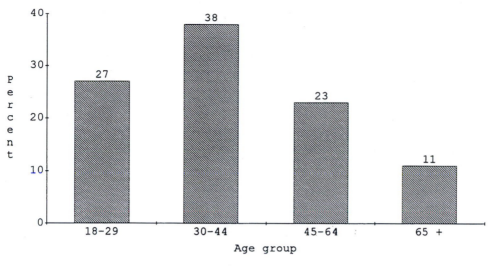

Figure 2-3.

Continuous and Discrete Measures

The results of measurement can be expressed as discrete values, or as values that are based on a continuous scale of measurement. Continuous measures are numbers. Discrete measures are labels that often express the result of some form of measurement. Discrete values are expressed on scales that are segmented rather than continuous. Nominal scale measurements are nearly always expressed as discrete values such as male and female, left and right, or correct versus incorrect. Ordinal scale measurements are often expressed as discrete values but may be based on an underlying continuous scale. Ranking students in terms of their school performance produces a discrete "class rank" value, but the rank is really a symbol of continuous measurement. The continuous measurement in this case is usually grade point average. Interval and ratio scale measurements are based on continuous scales and are nearly always expressed as such. Discrete values are useful because they are easier to interpret than continuous values. Continuous values, on the other hand, are useful because they are numerical and can be treated as such. Determining school performance, for example, is quicker and easier using the class rank than the grade point average. The convenience of the class rank value comes at a cost, however, because the performance of the individual student cannot be examined.

Let's consider an example that will summarize the basic ideas behind the scales of measurement. The grade earned in a course is probably a relevant result of measurement—especially to the person who earned it! How is the grade assigned? In most cases in the United States, grades are recorded in symbols: A signifies the best performance, B signifies good, C an average performance, and so on. By custom and habit, we attribute general characteristics of student performance to these letter grades and, perhaps frighteningly, often use them to make important decisions about people's futures. What scale of measurement do these letter grades illustrate? Is there the same distance between grades of A and B as between C and D? It's difficult to know for sure, but probably not. We know that letter grades are ordinal scale values but with the acknowledgment that they may be determined by many means. As a result, there can't be much certainty in distinguishing between any two grades on the same basis. We use the letters to signify performance, which often also implies how each student's performance ranked within a class of students. The letters are a shorthand way to describe academic performance. Curiously, though, we often arrive at these letter grades by using interval scale measures of other performances (tests, papers, presentations, etc.). Interval scale measures of such performances are summarized (averaged, commonly) and reported as letter grades. As we pointed out before, these letter grades are ordinal scale values and are less precise than the measures from which they are derived! To compound this situation, it is customary to then assign a numerical value to the letter grades on a four-point scale: four points for an A, three for a B and so on, and calculate an average of the grade points over each school term and entire training programs. This system is a ratio scale of measurement because zero points are given for failing grades. (These averages are called many things, including "grade point average" and "quality point average.") How precise can these overall averages be? Logically, measurement can only be as precise as its least precise component. Grade point averages, therefore, can only be as precise as the processes used for assigning the letter grades.

The point of all this discussion about scales of measurement is that evaluation only makes sense when the intended use matches level of measurement. To make these two match, you need to think ahead to what type of information you will need to make your evaluation meaningful, what type of measurement is likely to get you the information you need, and how you can analyze the information appropriately to get the answers.

THE ROLE OF MEASUREMENT IN EVALUATION

Measurement is an important part of practice in many professions. What is measured, and how, often depends on the discipline and the situation. Regardless, the design of methods to carry out measurement and the correct interpretation of results hinges largely on the level of measurement used.

In straightforward terms, evaluation can be defined as the comparison of observed values to a standard of comparison. Measurement is the means that provides us with the observed values, which is the information needed to decide whether the results were better, no different, or poorer than expected.

Measurement as a Tool for Evaluation

Evaluation of health education and health promotion is usually focused on the extent to which a predetermined and, hopefully, well-defined outcome was reached. Measurement is basic to this process. In most cases, numbers are used to provide information needed for evaluation. Let's consider a hypothetical example. Suppose you were in a work setting where your patients had suffered recent myocardial infarctions (heart attacks). Your program is designed to teach patients how best to use various methods for rehabilitation, thus helping them to recover as quickly as possible. If they follow the program's advice they should also have a much lower risk of having more heart attacks. How would you know if the program was successful? One approach to such an evaluation would be to examine the program design and compare the day-to-day operations with the activities that were planned. Did the activities occur as planned? Another approach would be to focus on the goals and objectives of the program. Were those goals and objectives accomplished? If one of the goals was to increase longevity of the patient, for example, then we could measure progress by keeping track of how long the patients lived. (Hopefully, we would not have to select a criterion that could include the influence of so many forces other than the program activities. It would be better to focus on indicators of how well the patients learned and used what the program was trying to teach.) Finally, we might also choose to assess the patients' self-confidence with exercise, or their general sense of well-being to determine the extent to which the program was helpful. Regardless of the approach, measurement would be an integral part of our evaluation. Each situation would present us with a different set of measurement challenges.

The purpose of this chapter has been to introduce the basic concepts that are involved with measurement. We are constantly measuring things in our environment every day of our lives, but most of our efforts are based on habit and intuition (if you go through a low door and don't bump your head, it was because you measured the height of the opening correctly). Evaluation relies on measurement that is planned and hopefully objective. The chapter that follows will address the accuracy of, measurement; the next chapters discuss specific issues related to measurement of knowledge, attitudes and behaviors.

READINGS

Cook, T.D., and Campbell, D.T.: *Quasi-Experimentation: Design and Analysis Issues for Field Settings.* Boston, Houghton Mifflin, 1979.

Ghiselli, E.E., Campbell, J.P., and Zedeck, S.: *Measurement Theory for the Behavioral Sciences.* San Francisco, Freeman, 1981.

Stevens, S.S.: Measurement. In Churchman, C.W. (Ed.): *Measurement: Definitions and Theories.* New York, Wiley, 1959.

Chapter Three

ASSESSING THE ACCURACY OF MEASUREMENT

For measurement to be useful, it must be accurate and to allow for communication, it must be reproducible. That is, measurement must be able to produce correct information and do so in a consistent and reliable manner. Understanding these two ideas, accuracy and reliability are critical to understanding measurement.

By accuracy we mean the extent to which measurements correctly describe what we want to measure. This issue of accuracy is very important and also somewhat complex. To begin, let's introduce some terms and concepts. To make the terms easier to deal with, consider an example. Suppose that you wanted to figure out how much knowledge clinic patients had about the organization of the health care system that they belong to. You are concerned about this issue because you sense that your personnel are spending too much of their time dealing with routine tasks and, furthermore, you suspect that a well-designed pamphlet would answer a lot of the questions and save you time. Before you can design the pamphlet, however, you need to develop a clear sense of the gaps in patient understanding. A simple, short questionnaire ought to provide you with enough information to design your pamphlet. But before you plunge into the design of the questionnaire, consider the information that you need and are likely to get. To do a good job designing your pamphlet, you will need information that accurately depicts the current level of understanding of your patients. At the same time you should realize that you will not be able to ask all the questions that are necessary to have an absolutely complete measurement of patients' understanding. That is, there will be measurement error in your assessment. You won't be able to take much of the patients' time, some of them won't understand all of the questions that you ask, and some will arrive at different interpretations of what you are asking. Some may answer in ways that express their respect and admiration for the health care professionals, while others may answer in ways that express their disappointment or anger. Because of these reasons (and be sure that there are many others), the results that you get with your questionnaire may be less than 100% accurate.

To cope with the inaccuracies that you may get in the responses to your questionnaire (and understand that you will not be able to uncover all of the problems), you need to interpret the results with caution. But how much caution? The amount of caution needed in interpreting data from the questionnaire depends on four characteristics of your questionnaire: its validity, reliability, usability and sensitivity. The term **validity** refers to the extent to which your questionnaire measures what you intended it to measure. A questionnaire with a high degree of validity is one that includes items that are able to correctly measure the knowledge of the clinic patients. A **reliable** questionnaire is one that stimulates answers from the clinic patients in a consistent fashion. That is, patients respond to each of the items in the same way, not with the same answer necessarily, but using the same thought processes. A questionnaire with a high degree of **usability** is one that is constructed and presented to the clinic patient so that they can answer the questions without confusion. A usable questionnaire is also one that you can administer and process readily. Confusing answer systems, technical language, complicated directions, and designs where the patients have to skip items are all examples of factors that make some questionnaires less usable. A **specific** instrument is one that collects information that is directly relevant to the evaluation questions that you have.

VALIDITY

As stated earlier, the term validity describes the extent to which an instrument measures as intended. Let's examine this statement in detail. When we state that a valid instrument measures as intended, we are implying that there is a definite plan that serves as a basis for the instrument and, furthermore, that an instrument is necessary to carry out measurement. For our purpose here, we can define instrument as any device that we use to organize what our senses perceive. For example, a tape measure is an instrument that we can use to organize what we sense about an object into statements about the object's size—its length, width, breadth, or distance from another object—into an organized system of measurement. The utility of the tape measure is that it is a valid, reliable, usable measurement tool. The results from the tape measure can be used to make specific statements about objects and their relation to other things in the environment, to reproduce the measurements in other ways, or for any other purpose. The tape measure is an instrument that can be used to convert our perceptions into precise statements. It is an instrument that allows conversion of perceptions into standardizable units. An IQ test does the same thing as the tape measure but instead of focusing on tangible objects, the IQ test attempts to measure an abstract concept. Instruments that measure knowledge, attitudes, behaviors, length, width, weight, etc., all do essentially the same thing. They convert various types of unorganized information into standard units that can be communicated. As we stated previously, a valid instrument measures as intended. What do we mean by intended? Intention implies a plan for measurement. An instrument can only be valid in terms of some clear purpose. A tape measure does not measure intelligence.

Just as there are a variety of situations requiring measurement, there are a variety of applications of the concept of validity. Validity of an instrument may be related to a criterion (a standard, in other words), or to some abstraction, or to specific content. As it turns out, these are types of validity.

Criterion-Based Validity

Criterion-based validity is derived from explicitly stated criteria that are the basic motivation for having a particular instrument. For example, licensing examinations for dentists in the United States include the mechanics of dental practice. In order to become licensed as a dentist, a person must pass an exam that includes both written and practical components. Dentists and licensing boards have agreed that there are minimal skills that dentists must be able to demonstrate for the public to be protected and served. The examination is based on dental skills that are used in everyday practice, and it has been accepted that successful demonstration of these skills is one of the criteria for being a licensed dentist. The dental licensing examination has criterion-based validity precisely because it is based on everyday activities involved in dental practice. To repeat, the criteria for the examination are the everyday skills needed for dental practice; the examination shows criterion-based validity because it requires demonstration of competence in these skills. An important feature of this type of validity is that it is based on judgment. The criteria are selected, by experts usually, to be representative of the desired outcome (being a good dentist), and the examination is derived from the criteria. The matter of judgment is very important for criterion-based validity. The selection of criteria is critical, since in most situations all criteria cannot be included in the licensing exam. Only those criteria that are believed to be most likely to be indicative of the outcome may be included. Returning to the dental examination example, what would be risked if the exam did not include the demonstration of skills? Is it possible that a dental school graduate could know all about dentistry and not be able to perform competently? The licensing boards believe that it is possible, and so the performance part of the examination is included. Criterion-based validity is based on specific standards for performance. An instrument is said to have criterion-based validity when it includes assessment of the criteria. This type of validity assumes that the selected criteria are representative of the outcome to be measured by the instrument.

Criterion-based validity can be subdivided into two categories: concurrent and predictive. Both of these terms address the time framework for the testing in question. Concurrent validity is concerned with valid measurement of what is true now, while predictive validity is focused on valid prediction of the future. When we speak of validity we are usually thinking about some frame of reference that has to do with time: the past, now, or at some time in the future. Tests that have to tell us something about right now are based on a different set of ideas than those that are intended to predict something about the future.

Concurrent Validity

An instrument with concurrent validity is one that accurately assesses the current status of the person being measured. Its validity isn't based on the past or the future of the individual, but focuses on the present. The criteria used to establish this type of validity must be currently observable, naturally. If a unit on AIDS had been recently discussed in a health education course, for example, then a test on the information that was included in the unit might be said to have concurrent validity. Claiming concurrent validity would be based on the notion that the test only measured what students knew about AIDS at this point in time. We would not be concerned with making statements about what the students might learn or how they might behave in the future, because our focus is on their current status.

Predictive Validity

Predictive criterion-related validity focuses on the future. An instrument with predictive validity is one that measures characteristics that are believed to be related to future behaviors. Such an instrument may focus on behavior, attitude development or capacity for learning, but the point is that the validity hinges on the instrument's ability to accurately measure the future. Validity can only be determined by seeing if the predictions are borne out.

It may be useful to summarize criterion-related validity with an example. Remember, criterion-related validity means just what it says: The validity of the measurement depends on how it compares to (external) criteria. Pretend that you are a basketball coach. When tryouts begin, you watch potential players go through drills in an effort to determine which have the best skills. The best passers, dribblers and shooters are impressive because it is obvious that those skills indicate which players have the best abilities. The judgment that you make of the players as they go through their drills and exhibit their skills is based on criteria that you believe are indicative of basketball skills. But remember, the goal is to find those who can learn to play well together as a team in competition. To the extent that what you decide to look for are valid indicators of real basketball skill (whatever that may be), your drills are concurrently valid. But you are having tryouts because you want to choose players that will be part of a winning team. Watching the players' skills in a non-game situation may or may not tell you anything about their abilities to play on a team, much less under "game" pressure. Through experience, you have found that some players who don't have outstanding skills, as they demonstrate in tryout drills, are able to play very well on a team. Furthermore, you have discovered that some players are "practice players" and that their outstanding practice performances mysteriously disappear during a real game. All of this points to the idea that maybe you shouldn't be too impressed by any players' skills on drills alone, but that you need to get some evidence of how they are likely to play in game situations. In other words, you need a test with predictive validity. So you divide the players into teams and have them scrimmage to get an idea of how well they might play on a team. To summarize, when you watch the players demonstrate their skills in drills, the accuracy of your judgment is based on concurrent validity and may not predict how the players will perform in a game. The scrimmage is intended to judge how well the players can be expected to play in a game, and its worth is based on predictive validity. Where do the criteria for all these judgments come from? In the case of the basketball team tryouts they come from experience, but they could also come from any number of sources. You might believe that to be successful, players should be of a specific minimum height, be able to react in a given time, or "hustle." The criteria are for you to choose. In many instances of criterion-related validity, the criteria are selected based on research, but just as often the criteria are selected on experience or guesses.

Construct Validity

Although the discussion of criterion-related validity may leave you with the impression that good criteria may satisfy most types of situations where validity is an issue, there is a need for additional approaches to establishing validity. Suppose there are no criteria that make sense to use for instrument validation. Suppose too that the instrument is trying to measure a quality about a person or situation that is really more of an abstract idea than a discrete criterion of performance. Imagine trying to develop criteria for a concept such as "helplessness." You could arbitrarily decide to choose something such as seeking help to stop smoking as a criterion for helplessness, but that may or may not make any sense. There are no clear criteria that always point to behaviors or attitudes that we would call "helplessness." Nevertheless, observant people know that helplessness exists, and they know it when they see it regardless of their ability to give it a measurable description. Such ideas that we commonly observe but are unable to attach to criteria can be called **constructs**. A construct is a term or phrase that labels a "theme" that we are unable to describe with any greater precision. Helplessness is an example of a construct. Self-concept and alienation are two other examples. If you are an observant, practical person, you will no doubt note that there are many constructs, particularly if you consider people's behaviors, and virtually none of them can be tied to clear, non-ambiguous behaviors (criteria). For example, someone that you might label as having a poor self-concept might exhibit any number of behaviors or attitudes that would make you think that they doubt their abilities. In all probability, your assessment of their self-concept will be based on the mixture of impressions that you develop based on interactions with that person and not from a single episode. The idea of a "construct" is to communicate that totality of impressions using a term or short phrase. All of this is well and good except when measurement comes into the picture. How can you measure something that we all agree is based on a totality of impressions? Everyone has a slightly different set of impressions!

An instrument can be said to have construct validity when it measures a construct as intended. What does the phrase "measures a construct as intended" mean? To have a valid measure we must have an instrument that taps the elements of the construct in a way that is acceptable. This is pretty vague and, as you might imagine, this is not an easy task. Construct validity is not simple to achieve and demonstrate. The most intuitive approach to construct validity (and the approach that makes the most sense) is to compare measurement of the new construct with a construct that you already believe in. Such an approach requires clear definitions of both the new construct and previously validated constructs. As long as you are willing to accept the definition and validity of some construct that is already "known," then you have a benchmark to use in validating your new construct. Based on theory, a conceptual relationship between established constructs and your new construct can be postulated. As your new construct is similar or different from the established one, so should the results of your measurement be. The technical terms for these possibilities are discriminant and convergent (construct) validity.

Convergent validity is demonstrated when the results of measuring the construct agree with results of measuring elements that should correlate with the construct, according to theory. Divergent validity, on the other hand, is demonstrated when the results of measurement of the construct differ with results of measurement of elements when theory says that they should differ. Consider an example. Suppose we were concerned with determining the validity of an instrument designed to measure "fear of cancer" to collect information on why people may avoid cancer screening tests. An instrument with 35 items is used, and the scoring is set up to show higher scores as fear of cancer increases. Preliminary research carried out within the target population showed that for many people, the sad experiences of their families, friends and co-workers had led them to believe that a diagnosis of cancer is a death sentence. Quite naturally, these people are likely to be fearful with any mention of cancer. The procedures for demonstrating convergent and divergent validity of the "fear of cancer" instrument would include administering the instrument to a group of people similar to those in the target population, and recording their experiences with cancer and other diseases in addition to their scores on the instrument. If the "fear of cancer" instrument is valid, then the instrument scores should vary according to experience with cancer, and those with high scores on the instrument should be those with the most experience with cancer. Figure 3-1 illustrates how we would expect scores on our "fear of cancer" scale to vary with experience with cancer. As Figure 3-1 shows, the scores on the scale are higher for those with more experience with cancer (converge). The scores also show a fluctuating pattern among those with little or no experience with cancer (divergence).

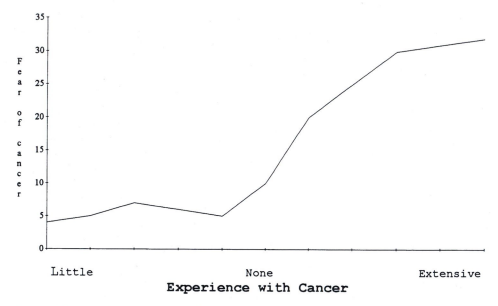

Figure 3-1. Fear of cancer is related to the amount of previous experience with the disease.

Little   →   →   →   Extensive
Experience with Cancer

Content Validity

The final type of validity that we will discuss is also the simplest. An instrument demonstrates content validity when it represents a body of information, usually knowledge, in a way that will provide for valid measurement. This usually involves the question about whether the instrument represents the content appropriately, covering the important components with the right depth. A simple example of the use of content validity is with the question of validity of the written tests that are commonly used for issuing drivers' licenses. A valid test would be one that samples the rules of driving with the appropriate breadth and depth.

Basic Rules Governing Validity

1. A valid test measures as intended.
2. The extent to which a test "measures as intended" can best be verified through collection of information or through logical extension of theory that underlies that which is to be measured.
3. When validity is established through collection of information, we call it "criterion-related." The time that elapses between the administration of the test and collection of information or observations for validation determines whether the criterion-related validity is concurrent or predictive.
4. Concurrent (criterion-related) validity is based on the here and now.
5. Predictive (criterion-related) validity is based on the test predicting the results of future performance.
6. Validation of some tests cannot be attached to criteria that exist in the real world; rather, these tests are intended to measure a theme or idea. These themes or ideas are called "constructs." Self-concept, locus of control, and anxiety are examples of constructs.
7. Construct validity involves demonstrating that the test measures enough components of the construct with sufficient depth to develop a reasonable estimate of its occurrence. This process is subjective and not based on clear, predetermined criteria.
8. Technically, construct validity is demonstrated using other known constructs. Theory tells us how self-concept may be related to locus of control, so if we have a supposedly valid measure of one we can use it to estimate the validity of the other. This is accomplished by convergent or discriminant validity and/or multitrait-multimethod approaches.
9. Convergent and divergent validity are based on the idea that two things that are essentially the same should be measured in

essentially the same way—i.e., the measurement of them should converge. Conversely, two things that are very different should not be measured in the same way, and similar measurement should yield very different (divergent) results.

10. Content validity is based on the extent to which an instrument measures a specific body of information (knowledge, usually) appropriately. An instrument with content validity samples the content appropriately.

RELIABILITY

We have just completed discussing validity: the extent to which an instrument measures as intended. There is another component to measurement accuracy, though, and that is reliability. In a word, reliability means consistency. A reliable instrument measures in the same way in each situation. If we are talking about students, patients, or subjects in an experiment, a reliable instrument would measure in the same way regardless of the individual characteristics of the person measured. As with validity, reliability is not a yes/no issue but rather a "to what extent" issue. In addition (and perhaps maddeningly), some instruments are highly reliable in some situations but unreliable in others.

Before we get too far into this discussion of reliability we need to take an important sidetrip into theoryland. There are two basic theories regarding the reliability of measurement: classical test theory and domain sampling. Classical test theory assumes that for every quality or quantity measured there is some underlying (and usually unknown) "true" value. Because of imprecision in measurement due to human error, uncontrollable environmental occurrences, inappropriateness of measurement instruments and other unanticipated things, the results that we get from measurement usually differ from the hypothetical "true" value. Furthermore, measurement error (differences between the true value and what we get) may be either systematic or unsystematic.

Result of Measurement = True Score + Error

Systematic error comes from things that can become known, and we can account for their influence in the results of measurement. Differences in intelligence, for example, will certainly influence results from achievement tests taken by elementary school children. Such differences are called systematic because we can understand and account for their influence. Unsystematic errors are just the opposite from systematic errors. We usually don't know about or understand unsystematic errors in measurement, so we cannot possibly account for their influence in the results. Recalling our initial definition of reliability, unsystematic errors reduce the reliability of measurement because they are inconsistent. Any factor that adds inconsistency to measurement threatens reliability. A subtle but important point to see in all of this is that classical test theory assumes that what you are measuring is a clearly defined entity, something that can be observed without much doubt, like your height or weight or how many square inches are on this page.

Classical test theory is somewhat limited by the assumptions about what is measured. In the social and behavioral sciences, we rarely (very rarely) measure anything discrete. Most of the important things are measured by putting together items that sample parts of a whole. This idea gives rise to the notion of "domain sampling" as an approach to measurement. A "domain" is the set of all of the elements that are considered part of a particular area of interest. For example, the domain for a test that a group of students are given on the cardiovascular system would be all of the information that **could** have been included on the test. The test is a sample from the domain. Nearly all measurement in health education and health promotion involves domain sampling because it is impractical, and usually impossible, to measure everything in the domain. In such situations we have to sample from a domain that we would like to measure. In practical terms, this "domain sampling" point of view doesn't have much impact in the mechanics of measurement but has a great deal to do with interpretation. The systematic and unsystematic error concepts are the same except that the sources of error are increased because of sampling. Whenever we sample, there is error because all elements in the domain are not included in the measurement.

Given the fact that there is error in measurement, regardless of whether we choose to believe in classic test theory or domain sampling, we need to have ways of estimating and documenting the error. Reliability theory gives us the means to explore error in the consistency of measurement. There are four common methods for determining the reliability of measurement: test-retest, parallel forms, split halves and internal consistency. Studying the means for testing reliability also provides a good explanation for the concept of reliability. Consequently, the sections that follow will discuss the most common methods for determining reliability. The test-retest method is applicable to many different situations. Parallel forms, split halves and internal consistency are somewhat limited in application compared to test-retest and are most commonly used for exploring reliability of written tests and inventories. (Methods for computing reliability are included in the Technical Appendix at the end of this chapter.)

Test-Retest

Test-retest is perhaps the most intuitive approach to establishing reliability. If you wanted to establish the consistency of some measuring device, you would probably come up with the idea of test-retest by yourself. It makes sense that a consistent, reliable measuring device should be able to measure the same thing repeatedly and get similar, if not duplicate, results. Conversely, if an instrument is used twice in the same way and we get different results, then something is wrong. Either the instrument is inconsistent or the thing that is being measured changes, or both. There is a problem in any case. It is perfectly obvious that we can't be sure of our instrument if we don't get consistent results. Test-retest reliability is carried out by administering a test at one point in time and then by repeating the same test in the same way to the same people again at a later time. As long as we're measuring something that is relatively stable, we should get very similar results on both administrations if our instrument is reliable. How much time should elapse between measurements? If we are administering a test of knowledge, then there is a good chance that the subjects will remember the items from the first time they took the test if we don't wait long enough before the retest. If this were to happen, we wouldn't know whether the test and retest scores were similar or different because they remembered, and gave the same answers based on their memory of the first time they took the test, or whether they reacted to the test the same way both times. To avoid this situation the administrations of the test and retest should be separated by enough time to reduce specific memory of the first testing and the answers given. On the other hand, if too much time elapses, the true score of the individual may change. The judgment of the proper amount of time is subjective and depends on the nature of the test and what it is designed to measure, the extent of change ongoing in the environment of those being tested and how much change may interfere with memory of the test and, finally, how much time may elapse before subjects are lost to follow-up. As a general rule, the more complex and detailed the test, the shorter the time needed between administration of test and retest. Two weeks' delay between administrations is a commonly used rule of thumb.

Parallel Forms

Parallel forms reliability involves construction of two equivalent versions of the same instrument. This method is generally limited to use with written instruments. If the results of measurement using the two instruments on the same people are the same, then the instruments are considered reliable. The advantage of parallel forms is that there is no worry about carryover from test to retest since the test forms are different. The disadvantage, of course, is that you have to have two equivalent forms of the test.

Split Halves

Split half reliability is an interesting concept. The basic idea is that two halves of a test, assuming that the items are well-mixed, should not be different in the response that they elicit from the subject. In other words, the responses to the test should be about the same on both halves of the test. Errors of measurement should be about equally divided between the halves of the test. Applying this concept to the problem of establishing reliability is very simple. Using only one administration of the test, the items are divided into two groups and scored. A highly reliable test should yield comparable results on the two halves. The items are usually assigned to the two groups by giving those with even numbers to one group, and those with odd numbers to the other. Occasionally, it makes sense to divide items into groups in other ways, the first half to one group and the second half to the other, but the point is to divide the items into groups in a way that makes the groups comparable. The idea of split halves can be extended to another form of reliability, sometimes called "component" reliability. In component reliability, separate components of the test are separated out and scored separately. Assuming that the components are of comparable difficulty, the scores should be similar for each component. The index of reliability for split halves is the correlation between the scores on each half of the test (or among the components of the test). If the correlation is high, 0.8 or better, then the test is believed to be reliable. Lower correlation coefficients suggest that those taking the test did not react consistently. The Technical Appendix at the end of this chapter includes detail on calculation of the correlation coefficient needed to carry out split half reliability.

Internal Consistency

The internal consistency method of estimating reliability is based on the relationship between results from each item and the total score. In essence, reliability is established by correlating the results from each item, whether the answer was correct or incorrect, with the total score. Items correlating positively with the total score indicate that those answering correctly tended to get higher total scores. Positive correlations support reliability. When an item correlates negatively with the total score, on the other hand, this means that the total score and the trend in answering the item were going in opposite directions. Those with higher scores tended to answer this item incorrectly, or those with lower scores tended to answer the item correctly. Negative correlations are usually an indication that there is confusing wording in the item or the scoring is incorrect. Reliability determined using the internal consistency method is reported using Cronbach's alpha (α). The computational method for this statistic is included in the Technical Appendix at the end of this chapter.

USABILITY AND SPECIFICITY OF MEASUREMENT

The final topics for this chapter are sometimes assumed to be obvious. Not only are they not obvious, but the fact that many consider them so means that many instruments are not as useful as they might be. These two topics deal with the applications for which the instrument has been developed. Usability is the ease with which the instrument can be used to collect the desired information from the people you want to measure. Specificity is the extent to which the instrument measures as intended within the context of the immediate purposes. Usable and specific instruments have acceptable levels of validity and reliability, of course, but they are also attuned to the characteristics of the target population given the information that is needed. Reliable and valid instruments to measure self-concept exist in great number, for example. Many of these instruments require reading ability and ability to deal with abstract thought, and would not be appropriate for people who can't read well or handle abstract ideas. On the other hand, instruments may match the capabilities of the target population nicely, but not be able to produce information about self-concept as it may relate to specific situations. Do you think that you would be able to apply the results of a general self-concept assessment to a health care environment? Perhaps, but unless the items were pertinent to the health care environment, you would have to assume that self-concept transferred across all environments and that the method of measurement didn't really matter. Such an assumption would take a lot of courage! It would make more sense to have a self-concept measure that was designed for the environment, and would be certain to tap those aspects of health care that might influence how people feel about themselves as patients. It would also be best to have an instrument that was appropriate to the skills and level of awareness of the patients. Finally, having a self-concept scale that could summarize "health care related feelings about self" would eliminate making assumptions about the impact of specific environments.

Specificity and usability can have dramatic impact on the validity and reliability of measurement. Lack of specificity most commonly affect validity by altering the extent to which the instrument measures as intended. An instrument that is insensitive to the context (one that does not consider the environment, for example) will not be able to measure accurately. An instrument that has low usability (one with directions that are too complicated for the patients, for example) introduces unsystematic error. Recall that unsystematic error reduces reliability of measurement.

In thinking about usability and specificity of measurement, consider the following:

1. How long will it take individuals in my target population to respond to my instrument? Will it take so long that they will get bored? Will it take so long that other activities (clinic schedules, for example) will be disrupted?
2. Is it practical for use in my setting? Will it apply to all of the people in the target population? Is it realistic for my setting in terms of time and equipment needed?
3. Can the administration of the instrument be standardized? Do the directions require interpretation? Could people other than you administer the instrument?
4. Is the instrument appropriate for the lives of the clients? Is it

written at the appropriate level of language? Does it require reading skills beyond the average level for the clients? Is it written in a way to hold the attention of the clients?

5. Can the instrument be scored to give the information that is wanted? Will the information be easy or difficult to summarize? Are there good reasons for asking each question?

These questions may help you to examine the usability and specificity of a measurement instrument. As you can see, usability and specificity are not technical issues, they are issues of common sense. A usable and specific instrument is one that can collect the information you need from the people in a way that is interesting and well matched to them.

This chapter has introduced the concepts of validity and reliability of measurement, usability and specificity. Valid measurement is accurate; it measures as intended. Reliable measurement is consistent. Usability and specificity are two characteristics of measurement that have to do with application. Usable and specific measurement is attuned to the needs and capabilities of the target population and also gives results that directly serve the purpose of the measurement.

READINGS

Cronbach, L.J.: Coefficient alpha and the internal structure of tests. *Psychometrika, 16:*297–334, 1951.

Cronbach, L.J.: *Essentials of Psychological Testing,* 3rd ed. New York, Harper & Row, 1970.

Lien, A.J.: *Measurement and Evaluation of Learning,* 3rd ed. Dubuque, Brown, 1976.

Richardson, G.F., and Kuder, M.: The theory of the estimation of test reliability. *Psychometrika, 2:*135–138, 1937.

SPSS, Inc.: *User's Guide: SPSSX.* New York, McGraw-Hill, 1983.

Carmines, E.G., and Zeller, R.A.: *Reliability and Validity Assessment.* Beverly Hills, Sage, 1979.

TECHNICAL APPENDIX

TOOLS FOR MEASURING ACCURACY AND RELIABILITY

In this chapter we have discussed the concepts that form the foundation for assessing the accuracy of measurement. In this appendix, we will present some of the techniques that can be used to produce numerical expressions of the accuracy of measurement. The materials that follow are organized into three sections: summarizing results of measurement, assessing the accuracy of measurement, and assessing reliability. The first section, measures of central tendency and dispersion, presents some of the most commonly used descriptions of measurement. The second section of the appendix discusses measures used to estimate the accuracy of measurement, and the third section reviews techniques used in evaluating reliability. For simplicity of language, we will refer to all measurement instruments in this section as "tests." Remember, however, that measurement can be carried out with many different instruments and not just tests.

Summarizing Measurement

Suppose you gave a group of 42 secondary school students a 70-item, multiple-choice test to gauge their knowledge about prevention of heart disease before beginning a unit on the subject. The scores, the total number of items answered correctly, are summarized in Figure 3a-1.

How would you describe the performance of the 42 students on the test shown in Figure 3a-1? There are a number of different ways to answer to this question, but by using descriptive statistics, including measures of "central tendency," we can describe the results from the test in an efficient manner. Descriptive statistics include basic information about the test and the students, as well as summary measures of the students' performance. The summary measures include the mean, median, mode, range, variance and standard deviation. The mean, median and

Test Score	Frequency
42	1
43	2
44	3
45	5
46	6
47	7
49	6
50	5
51	4
57	2
63	1
Total 2015	42

Figure 3a-1. Frequency Distribution of 42 Test Scores

mode are also referred to as measures of "central tendency," while the range, variance and standard deviation are commonly known as measures of "dispersion."

Measures of Central Tendency

Mean. The mean is also known as the "average" and is used to represent the "typical" value in a set of data. The mean is calculated by summing the scores and dividing by the number of scores summed. It is important to recognize that while the mean is a useful statistic, it does not always represent the "typical" value. If there are extreme values among the data, the mean will be affected. For the test scores shown earlier in Figure 3a-1, the mean is as follows:

Mean score = Σscores ÷ number of scores = 2015 ÷ 42 = 47.97

Median. If we arranged a set of test scores in order from low to high, or high to low (the list of scores arranged in order is called an "ordered array"), the middle value would be the median. By definition, when there is an even number of observations, the median is between the two observations nearest the middle of the ordered array. The median is useful because it is quick to find and is not affected by extreme values like the mean. The median for the 42 test scores that we presented earlier would be halfway between the 21st and 22nd scores. As Figure 3a-2 shows, the median score is 47.

Mode. The mode is the observation that occurs most frequently. When more than one observation is repeated, more than one mode will occur. Figure 3a-3 shows that there are more scores of 47 than any other score.

Observation #	1	2	3	4	5	6	7	8	9	10	11	12	13	14	15	16	17	18	19	20	21	22
Score	42	43	43	44	44	44	45	45	45	45	45	46	46	46	46	46	46	47	47	47	47*	47
Observation #	23	24	25	26	27	28	29	30	31	32	33	34	35	36	37	38	39	40	42	42		
Score	47	47	49	49	49	49	49	49	50	50	50	50	50	51	51	51	51	57	57	63		

*Half of the scores are larger than the median and half are smaller. For the data shown above the median is halfway between the 21st and 22nd score. Since score 21 and 22 are both 47, the median is 47.

Figure 3a-2. An ordered array of test scores indicates that the median is exactly in the middle of the distribution of scores

Observation #	1	2	3	4	5	6	7	8	9	10	11	12	13	14	15	16	17	18	19	20	21	22
Score	42	43	43	44	44	44	45	45	45	45	45	46	46	46	46	46	46	47	47	47	47	47
Observation #	23	24	25	26	27	28	29	30	31	32	33	34	35	36	37	38	39	40	42	42		
Score	47	47	49	49	49	49	49	49	50	50	50	50	50	51	51	51	51	57	57	63		

Figure 3a-3. The 42 observations are arranged in order from lowest to highest. The mode is the most commonly occurring score.

Measures of Dispersion

In addition to measures of central tendency, we need to have measures of dispersion or "spread" of the data if we are to have a complete picture. The three most commonly used measures of dispersion are the range, variance and standard deviation.

Range. The range is the difference between the largest and smallest observation. The range is a crude measure of dispersion, but gives a quick picture of the data, and also serves a useful purpose in identifying errors and outliers. Unusually high or low values could be errors, mistakes in recording, scoring, or both. Outliers are values that are unexpectedly high or low, but are legitimate. In the set of test scores, the range would be 21 points, the difference between the highest score, 63, and the lowest, 42.

Variance. The variance is a measure of the spread of scores about the mean. The general formula for the variance is shown in Figure 3a-4.

$$s^2 = \frac{\sum (x_i - \overline{x})^2}{(n-1)}$$

Figure 3a-4. General Formula for the Variance.

To help with the notation used in Figure 3a-4, $\sum (x_i - \overline{x})^2$ means to subtract the mean, $\overline{x}$, from each test score, x_i, square the difference and total over all of the test scores.

For the test scores shown in Figure 3a-1, the calculation of the variance can be simplified to allow for more than one score with the same value. Figure 3a-5 illustrates the variance calculation for the test scores shown in Figure 3a-1.

Test Score	Frequency	(score-x⁻)	(score-x⁻)²	(score-x⁻)²*frequency
42	1	− 6	36	36
43	2	− 5	26	52
44	3	− 4	16	48
45	5	− 3	9	45
46	6	− 2	4	24
47	7	− 1	1	7
49	6	1	1	6
50	5	2	4	20
51	4	3	9	36
57	2	9	81	162
63	1	15	225	225
Total 2015	42		412	661

$$\text{Variance} = \Sigma \text{ (score} - x^-)^2 * \text{frequency} \div \text{(number of scores} - 1)$$
$$= 661 \div (42 - 1) = 16.12$$

Figure 3a-5. Calculation of the Variance for Grouped Scores

Standard Deviation. The standard deviation is the square root of the variance. The standard deviation is useful because it allows variation about the mean to be interpreted simply. The variance (s^2) is produced in squared units, which cannot be interpreted. Taking the square root of the variance produces a value that is interpreted in the same units as the test scores. Thus, the standard deviation (s) of the variance of the test scores, 16.12, is 4. The standard deviation, s, is interpreted in the same units as the mean of the test.

The standard deviation is also useful in providing information about the distribution of scores. As a general rule, about 2/3 (68.26%) of the scores are within one standard deviation of mean, 95% are within two standard deviations and 99.9% within three standard deviations of the mean. Any score within 1 standard deviation of the mean is typical of 2/3 of the scores. Scores that are between 1 and 2 standard deviations from the mean are either in the upper or lower 2.5% of scores, and those that are between 2 and 3 standard deviations away from the mean represent .05% of all of the scores. Figure 3a-6 illustrates the range of scores covered within 1, 2, and 3 standard deviations of the mean for the test scores that we saw earlier in Figure 3a-1.

```
|------------------------ 99%    ---------------------|
    |-------------- 95%    -------------|
        |---- 68%    ---|
  36       40       44       48       52       56       60
 -3s      -2s      -1s       x       +1s      +2s      +3s
```

Figure 3a-6. Percent of Data Included within 1, 2 and 3 Standard Deviations (s=4.0) of the Mean ($\bar{x}$=48)

Recall that the scores presented in Figure 3a-1 ranged from 42 to 63. Note that the range of scores shown in Figure 3a-5 for 2 and 3 standard deviations is beyond the range of the scores in the data set. This indicates that the distribution of scores is not symmetric about the mean, and the distribution is weighted slightly toward the upper end of the scale.

Knowing the measures of central tendency and dispersion provides us with the means of developing a quick picture of the distribution of the values. The mean identifies the "typical" value in the data set, the median identifies the middle of the data, and the mode shows the most commonly occurring value(s). The range shows whether there are likely to be extreme values that may distort the mean and the standard deviation. If we know the mean and standard deviation, we can also know where to expect 66%, 95% and 99% of the values to lie.

Correlation. Another basic statistic that is vital to the investigation of reliability is the correlation coefficient. Correlation is a term that is used to describe the extent to which information from two measurements varies in similar or different ways. Such data may vary in the same way (positive correlation), in opposite ways (negative correlation), or not vary in any recognizable pattern (no correlation). The basic form for determining the extent of correlation, Pearson's r, is shown in Figure 3a-7.

$$r = \frac{n(\Sigma x_i y_i) - (\Sigma x_i)(\Sigma y_i)}{\sqrt{n(\Sigma x_i^2) - (\Sigma x_i)^2}\sqrt{n(\Sigma y_i^2) - (\Sigma y_i)^2}}$$

Figure 3a-7. Formula for calculating Pearson's r.

where the xi's and yi's are the values obtained from two different measures on the same person. The values of r range from −1.00 to 1.00

and form the basis for interpreting the strength of correlation. In general, correlations above .80 indicate a strong relationship between the two measures. Correlations between .6 and .8 indicate a moderate relationship, and those between .4 and .6 are present but not strong. Correlations below .4 are usually judged to be weak or absent. It is important to remember, however, that judgment of correlation is dependent on the context. In areas of study with strict control over measurement, correlations below .7 may be considered weak or absent. Areas of study with uncertain measurement, on the other hand, may accept correlations of .4 as indicative of a strong relationship. To illustrate how the correlation coefficient works, let's examine the relationship between grade point averages and test results, using the information shown earlier in Figure 3a-1. Figure 3a-8 shows the test scores and the grade point averages (4.0 = A) for the students. Figure 3a-9 shows the relationship between the test scores and grade point averages in a scatterplot. Figure 3a-9 shows that low grade point averages and low test scores go together, and that the test scores tend to increase slightly as the grade point averages increase. The highest test scores were found among students with the highest grade point averages. The correlation between grade point average and test score turned out to be .77, which indicates a strong relationship.

Test Score	Frequency	Grade Point Averages						
42	1	2.0						
43	2	2.0,	2.3					
44	3	1.8,	2.2,	2.5				
45	5	1.8,	2.0,	2.0,	2.2,	2.5		
46	6	2.0,	2.0,	2.6,	2.8,	2.8,	3.0	
47	7	2.0,	2.0,	2.3,	2.5,	2.8,	3.1,	3.2
49	6	2.2,	3.0,	3.1,	3.1,	3.3,	3.4	
50	5	2.8,	3.0,	3.0,	3.1,	3.5		
51	4	3.0,	3.0,	3.2,	3.3			
57	2	3.5,	3.6					
63	1	3.8						
Total 2015	42							

Figure 3a-8. Frequency Distribution of 42 Test Scores and Grade Point Averages of the students

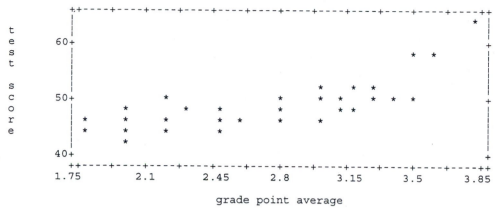

Figure 3a-9. Scatterplot of test scores and grade point averages.

Assessing Accuracy of Measurement

Now that we have some basic statistical tools, the mean, standard deviation, variance, and correlation coefficient, we can proceed to investigate a basic measure of instrument accuracy: the standard error of measurement. The standard error of measurement (SEM) is an estimate of how much variation we would expect in an individual's scores over a number of repetitions of the same test. This statistic is based on the assumptions that:

1. The individual possesses a hypothetical "true score" that is relatively stable over time.
2. Individual errors in measurement are completely random and not due to systematic things like reading ability or confusion about directions.
3. We can add the hypothetical "true score" and the estimate of unsystematic error and arrive at a valid "observed score" for the individual.

The form for determining the Standard Error of Measurement is shown in Figure 3a-10.

$$SEM = s_x\sqrt{1 - r_{xy}}$$

Figure 3a-10. General form of the Standard Error of Measurement.

where s_x is the standard deviation of the scores obtained on any administration of the test, and r_{xy} is the correlation of the test with a measure of a quality believed similar to that in question. Now let's look at an example to see how this approach might be used and, more importantly, see how the results might be interpreted.

Suppose we want to measure self-concept. We realize that any instrument that we choose will not measure self-concept exactly but will give us an estimate. (Why only an estimate? Because the instrument only gives us a sample of the "self-concept" domain.) The SEM will allow us to make a statement about the precision of our estimate. Using a self-concept scale that we developed, we obtain a mean and standard deviation, say 50 and 10. We know that the correlation between results from scale D and another much more complicated scale is .85. Using our formula for SEM, we get a result of 3.87. From the SEM, we know that the "true" measure of self-concept is 50, the mean of scale D, plus or minus the SEM; somewhere between 46.13 and 53.87. Statistical theory gives us more information about the precision of this estimate, though. We know that most of the time, 68% of the data are included within 1 standard deviation of the mean, 95% within two standard deviations, and 99.5% within three standard deviations. Since we used one standard deviation in our calculation of the SEM, we know that if we were to give the same self-concept scale to the same person repeatedly, her score would be within 46.13 and 53.87 about 68% of the time. A higher correlation between the scales, r_{xy}, will yield a smaller SEM, as will a smaller standard deviation of the scale used. In sum, the SEM expresses the precision of the measurement by giving upper and lower bounds on the observed score. The narrower the bounds, of course, the more accurate and reliable the scale.

Assessing Reliability

Remember that there are two basic approaches to reliability. The first approach relies on repetition of the test, with reliability being demonstrated when the performance of the test is consistent. The second approach looks inside the test, so to speak, and investigates consistency from item to item.

In focusing on the first approach to reliability, we'll consider the parallel forms and test-retest methods. In using **parallel forms**, the individual completes two versions of the instrument. Remember that the versions must be equivalent in every way. **Test-retest** uses the same instrument and individuals and administers the test on two different occasions. The concept underlying reliability testing is that the results obtained from one form should be very nearly identical to results obtained from the other. Using the correlation coefficient, the results obtained from both administrations are combined into one statement, the value of r. Generally speaking, correlation coefficients of less than .4 are considered not to represent any relationship between the tests. A value of .4 to .6 indicates a "slight" relationship, while a value of .6 to .8 represents a "moderate" relationship. Values of r above .8 indicate a "substantial" correlation. In general, the closer the correlation coefficient (r) is to 1.00, the greater the reliability.

Split half reliability also uses the correlation coefficient, but the correlation is between the scores obtained on each half of the test. Recall that the procedure for carrying out split half reliability is to administer the test and score each half (odd and even items, for example) of the test independently. The scores from the two halves of the test are then used in calculating the correlation coefficient. To adjust the correlation for interpreting the entire test, a correction known as the Spearman-Brown Prophesy formula, r_{sb}, is used. The Spearman-Brown Prophesy formula is shown in Figure 3a-11. In the Spearman Brown Prophesy formula, the correlation between the two halves of the test, r, is used in the denominator as well as the numerator.

$$r_{sb} = \frac{2r}{1+r}$$

Figure 3a-11. The Spearman-Brown Prophesy formula.

Internal consistency also uses the correlation coefficient but in a slightly different way. Cronbach's alpha (α), consistency, is calculated as shown in Figure 3a-12.

$$(\alpha) = \frac{k}{k-1} \left(1 - \sum \frac{s^2_{x_i}}{s^2_{x_t}}\right)$$

Figure 3a-12. Cronbach's Alpha.

where k is the number of items in the scale, s^2_{xi} are the variances for each item in the scale and s^2_{xt} is the variance of the total score. The interpretation of the alpha coefficient is the same as that of r, but by looking at the formula closely you can see that the idea behind Cronbach's alpha is quite different from the measures of reliability previously presented. Internal consistency is similar to split half reliability, but split half reliability was the correlation of summary scores between the two halves of the test. Cronbach's alpha improves on the split half concept by relating the variance of each item with the variance of the total score for all items on the test. This method allows comparison among the items on the test to determine the relative contribution of each item to reliability.

To illustrate how the internal consistency approach to reliability functions, consider an example of a 12-item test of knowledge of AIDS prevention. The test items are all multiple-choice with five choices. For internal consistency calculations, the procedure is to assign a value to each choice for each item. For this example, an answer of *a* was assigned a value of 1, *b* a value of 2 and so on, with *e* having a value of 5. From this structure, descriptive statistics were calculated for each item and for the total score, the number of items answered correctly. Figure 3a-13 shows the results of the calculations.

Item #	Item Mean	Item Variance	s^2_{xi}/s^2_{xt}
1	2.96	1.82	.04
2	3.94	1.42	.03
3	3.48	2.25	.05
4	3.96	1.17	.03
5	3.87	1.39	.03
6	3.26	1.06	.02
7	4.09	1.37	.03
8	3.87	0.79	.02
9	4.20	1.04	.02
10	4.31	0.90	.02
11	3.52	1.17	.03
12	2.72	.81	.02
Total	42.20	43.16	$\sum s^2_{xi}/s^2_{xt} = .33$

$$\alpha = \frac{12}{12-1}(1-.33) = .73$$

Figure 3a-13. Calculation of Cronbach's Alpha.

We can also test the reliability of a test in terms of whether individuals answered items correctly. The calculation of reliability is similar to the approach used in calculation of Cronbach's alpha. Figure 3a-14 shows the approach used for the Kuder-Richardson Formula # 20 (also known as the "KR20").

$$KR20 = \frac{k}{k-1} \, \frac{1 - \Sigma p_i q_i}{s^2},$$

Figure 3a-14. Calculation form for the KR20.

where p_i is the proportion answering item i correctly, $q_i = 1 - p_i$, s^2 is the variance of the test scores, and k is the number of items on the test. The interpretation of the KR20 is the same as for Cronbach's alpha. KR20 values of .80 or greater indicate that the test has good reliability.

Computer programs are currently available that can generate a variety of estimates of reliability including test-retest, split half, parallel forms, Cronbach's alpha and the KR20. (See the SPSS source listed in the references at the end of this chapter for details.)

Reliability estimates are interpreted in terms of the amount of error that is acceptable in the instrument. Recall that the basic notion guiding reliability is illustrated as follows:

True score = Test score + error

As the formula suggests, the smaller the error, the closer the test score will be to the true score. In general, reliability estimates from methods using correlation or alpha that turn out to be less than .80 ordinarily indicate that too much error exists, and we conclude that the instrument is not reliable. Low reliability may be associated with several correctable factors such as reading level of the test and clarity of instructions. When the reading level of the test is too high for the target population, reliability often suffers. Likewise, when wording of items or instructions for answering test items are open to interpretation, reliability will be reduced. For example, items using double negatives, such as "Which of the following factors are not associated with low risk heart disease?", may be answered with little consistency because the question being asked is unclear. In general, any factor that produces inconsistent responses to test items is likely to threaten reliability.

Chapter Four

SCALES, TESTS AND INDICES

The previous chapter discussed measurement from a conceptual point of view. Our next task is to take those ideas and put them to use in carrying out measurement. In this chapter we will cover the basic framework for development and testing of measurement instruments. When you've had time to digest the information, you should understand the concepts that are common to most of the types of instruments that you'll encounter. More detailed discussion of the development of instruments specifically for measuring knowledge, attitudes and behavior will come in the chapters that follow.

Most instruments that we use to measure knowledge, attitudes or behavior provide us with a sample of what we want to measure. This idea is very important and basic, one that you will encounter over and over again. To put some flesh on the bones of this idea of sampling, so to speak, try to remember a test that you have taken that measured everything you knew about a particular subject. Can you remember tests like that? Probably not. Tests sample what you know, and a good test samples in a way that provides an accurate representation of your knowledge. If you remember "bad" tests, tests that you thought didn't let you show what you knew, you might have thought they were bad because they didn't measure the subject matter with the right depth or breadth, in your judgment at least. The art of constructing measurement instruments is centered around somehow getting a mixture of items that not only assess the breadth of what you want to measure but also the depth. To try and meet this challenge, we need to develop measurement instruments (scales, tests, and indices) that not only meet the breadth and depth requirements but are also usable.

The terms scale, test, and index are names that are used to identify more or less specific types of measurement instruments. The distinction between these types of instruments has more to do with the motivation for having them than with their specific form.

What do we mean by the term "scale?" This term is used very commonly by social and behavioral scientists. The motivation behind using a scale is simply to collect information that describes an individual or group and be able to represent the information with a summarizing value or values (usually a number). On a practical level, scales can be described as sets of items that have been put together for the purpose of collecting information about particular characteristics of persons or groups. The term "scale" is often used very generally, though, and may refer to almost any type of measurement instrument.

A "test" is also a set of items put together for the purpose of assessment, but the motivation behind "testing" is to determine how much someone knows about a topic. Tests are also distinguished by the fact that there are definite "correct" responses to items. None of the other types of measurement instruments are designed with preconceived ideas of right and wrong answers to items.

An "index" is formed by combining characteristics that describe an individual or group. The characteristics may be purely descriptive, like occupation or income, or they may be the results of combinations of items from scales or tests. For example, "socioeconomic status" (SES, for short) is a phrase that is commonly used to describe one's "station in life." It is an index that is usually a combination of income, education and occupation. These three characteristics—income, education and occupation—all contribute to the description of one's "station in life," but none provides a complete picture of SES alone. By using a combination of all three, we get a much more complete description of SES, one that includes the contribution of all three factors. Depending on the circumstances, we may need the results provided by a single scale or test, an index, or some combination of the three.

CONSTRUCTING SCALES AND TESTS

The task of developing scales and tests consists of 10 basic steps:

1. Develop statements that describe what we want to measure.
2. Organize statements by priority, breadth, and depth.
3. Derive the essence of items using the statements.
4. Decide on the best response mode for the instrument.
5. Screen items' essence for contribution to the instrument.
6. Produce a rough draft of instructions for completion of the instrument.

7. Review scoring and processing procedures.
8. Pilot test the instrument.
9. Determine reliability and decide to revise or start over.
10. Develop a final draft of the instrument and pilot test.

Developing Items

Objectives: Sources of Items

Where do the items that make up scales and tests come from? This is a very basic and important question to ask. The answer depends on the nature of the measurement process. Let's consider some hypothetical situations that illustrate the wide variety of measurement processes.

• We want to measure how much the students in a health promotion course have learned during the first six weeks of the term.

• We want to measure "math phobia" among the students in a course on evaluation and measurement.

Although both of these situations involve measurement, there is a big difference between the two in terms of what is to be measured. What is the difference? In the first situation where we want to measure learning, based on teaching, we should have a clear idea of what to measure. The second situation is different, though. Although we may be able to sense that "math phobia" is common in students, and this may be part of the motivation for wanting to measure it in the first place, there is a definite difference between measuring what was "taught" and what was "sensed." What was "taught" is based on objectives, the objectives that are the basis for classroom teaching. What was "sensed" is not based on objectives but is a construct, or theme, that describes characteristics of an individual.

The use of objectives to guide measurement and evaluation is the cornerstone of scale and test development. Furthermore, when objectives are based on careful thought and are clearly stated, measurement and evaluation are much easier than when objectives are not developed with care. In trying to figure out how to measure teaching and learning and if there are no clear objectives, then the process should stop until objectives are developed. The exercise is good discipline; it helps teaching, and evaluation cannot be done without objectives anyway. References that will guide the process of developing objectives are at the end of the chapter.

Construct-Based Items

The measurement of knowledge is based on objectives, but what about the second situation where what we want to measure is not as clear-cut as "knowledge?" What is the basis of measuring a "construct?" Recall from the last chapter that a construct is a theme, like "math phobia." We recognize this condition when we see or experience it, but might not be able to clearly describe it in simple language. The only basis we have for developing a scale to measure "math phobia" is our conception of the characteristics of individuals who are suffering from it. Carefully developed, a list of such characteristics might provide a good basis for developing a scale. The factor that will determine whether a list of characteristics provides a good basis for evaluation or not is the extent to which the list represents an adequate sample of what we want to measure. We may be limited by our ability to imagine what "math phobia" is like and what the most common symptoms of sufferers might be. In addition, it is possible that there is considerable variation in "math phobia" and that what we now think of as one syndrome is really a group of related, but distinct conditions. Regardless, if we are to develop a scale that will measure "math phobia," then we have to decide upon a set of characteristics that will represent this condition accurately. These characteristics will form the basis for measurement, just as the objectives used for teaching are the basis for measurement of what was learned. We could also define an index that would combine the results of measuring learning and phobia and produce a summary measure of how much "math phobia" inhibits learning (maybe we could call it "phobia-induced learning inhibition" or something.) We would have to be careful in interpreting our index, though, being sure not to imply that the phobia caused problems with learning. The index would only produce a number that we could use to estimate the relationship between phobia and learning. We wouldn't know if the phobic response existed before the student tried to learn what was taught or not.

Organizing Statements into Items

Targets of Measurement

Up to this point we have established, in conceptual terms at least, that the basis for developing measurement instruments is a set of clear statements that describe what we want to measure. To generalize this idea, we can think of developing statements that fit into three different categories of targets for measurement: knowledge, attitudes, or behaviors. In nearly every case where we would want to use measurement, we can categorize what we want to accomplish into: (1) wanting to increase knowledge, (2) wanting to change attitudes or opinions, or (3) wanting to change behaviors. If the goal is to increase knowledge, then the statements can be derived from the objectives for teaching. For attitudes or opinions, which turn out to be treated as constructs (like "math phobia"), the statements are descriptions of the condition and its effects that are associated with the attitude or opinion. If the goal is to measure behavior, then the statements are the parts of the behavior in question. After reading these thoughts about specifying how knowledge, attitude or behavior change will be brought about, it should be clear that measurement and evaluation are greatly helped when objectives are specified before the education is begun. (While it might seem that we are beating a dead horse with all the references to objectives, it is probably more common for objectives to be developed after education has begun than before.)

Once a suitable set of objectives or descriptive statements has been developed, the next task is to organize the statements into a format to develop the instrument. When objectives are known, the issue of sampling becomes important. For most situations, it will become clear that, once objectives are written out, all objectives cannot be measured at the same breadth and depth. A basic, important decision to be made is which of the objectives need to be measured most carefully by using more items and which can be covered with fewer items. This decision should not be made too quickly, because the extent to which the instrument measures as intended depends in large part on how well the content area is sampled. Additionally, there are no hard and fast rules to guide this decision. A decision must be made regarding the most essential elements to include, and what depth each part of measurement should have.

Item Essence

Once the coverage of the topic has been worked out satisfactorily, the essence of each of the items can be generated. It is important to develop the items in parts; first developing the basic question to be answered (or statement put forth for reaction, if we're talking about a construct), then adding the response mode. (The "response mode" is the way the item will be answered.) Developing items in parts gives you the option of considering many different possibilities for the "type" of item.

Response Mode

The basic types of items include essay, short-answer, multiple-choice forms, true-false, checklists, semantic differentials, Likert scales, and so on. There are also many variations on these item types. The choice of item type depends on at least two factors. Initially, the information that you want to get from a particular item may require written expression. If so, then the essay or short-answer forms are indicated. At the same time, written expression is subject to interpretation, and if you want the scoring of the items to be unambiguous, then written expression item types are not a good idea. If scoring is a priority—fast, efficient and objective scoring is needed—then objective-type items are indicated. Remember that for attitude assessment we are interested in opinions rather than facts. Most of the time the response modes for attitude scales are such that the person completing the items has the opportunity to express agreement rather than deciding on "right or wrong."

Screening Items

When the items have been developed with the response modes, the initial screening can be started. Screening of items is an important, if tedious, task. Each of the items must be considered as a part of the total instrument. Does each item contribute to the whole in terms of similarity of language? Are all of the items using the same format worded in the same way? Is the language consistent from item to item? An initial screening of items in light of the total instrument is very likely to uncover subtle differences between types of items, idiosyncrasies of language, and other things that may distract or cause confusion.

Producing a Draft of the Instrument

When the initial screening is complete, the next step is to organize the items into a draft of the complete instrument. The first thing is to develop instructions for those who will be taking it. This may seem clear and easy, but be careful. The instructions are very important, especially for instruments that will be completed with little or no monitoring. The most important things to think about in developing instructions are the characteristics of the patients, clients, students or whomever will complete the instrument. How well can they read? Are they used to completing instruments like this? Do they all speak and read the same language, and is it the same as yours? Is the subject of your instrument likely to cause emotionally charged responses? Basically, it is wise to be as suspicious and skeptical about the reactions of people to your instrument as possible. Remember Murphy's most basic law (if anything can go wrong it will), and develop instructions as detailed as possible.

Developing Scoring Procedures

When a satisfactory first draft of the instrument has been developed, complete with instructions, then the next thing is to review the scoring and processing procedures. Do this step now! It's very common to save working out these "details" for later. Putting it off is a big mistake! The basic motivation for developing the instrument should guide this step. If you want to use the results to classify people, measure their knowledge, attitudes or behaviors or whatever, then you have to get clear on how you plan to get from a pile of completed instruments to the results wanted. Computer processing can make the repetitive parts of the task easier, but you still have to decide how to get the information from the instruments and into the machine and then get out what you want.

Pilot Testing

Pilot testing provides invaluable opportunities to learn about the validity, reliability, and usability of instruments. When you've convinced yourself that you have a good draft of the instrument and know how the results will be processed, then you can begin planning a pilot test. A pilot test is a "dry run." Your primary objective in doing a pilot test is to find out what is likely to happen when you use the instrument to collect the data you need. Anything that you have overlooked in creating the instrument will hopefully become apparent, and you can fix it without risk to your evaluation. The best pilot tests use people just like those you want to collect data from, but if you can't get such people then get as close as possible. Failing that, have honest colleagues and others serve as pilot test subjects.

Administer the instrument in the pilot test just as you plan to do with the "real" people. Simulate as much of the environment as you can, including noise and distractions, lighting, and so on. When the pilot subjects have finished, select a few and interview them about the instrument. Go over their responses and find out how they decided to answer as they did. Have all your senses keenly attuned to pick up everything they say and particularly their non-verbal reactions to the instrument. When you have finished, take all the completed instruments and process them exactly as you plan, computer and all. This process can be tedious and expensive but can also be a lifesaver. Look for things that you can do to improve the instrument, the processing, or even the whole project. Learn from your experience!

Estimating Reliability

The pilot test will give you completed instruments and impressions from the interviews. The interview impressions will let you know how clear the instructions and items were, and whether and where changes need to be made. The responses on the instruments themselves will allow you to calculate an estimate of reliability. (Cronbach's alpha is probably the best statistic for this task. Alternatively, split halves may be used.) The estimate of reliability is crucial for the future of the instrument. Reliability will lead you to make a basic decision. If the reliability is okay (review Chapter Three to see how to calculate reliability and interpret the result), then you can make necessary (cosmetic) changes and go on. If the reliability is suspect, then the changes are likely to be more fundamental and you'll need to make them and do the pilot over again. If the reliability is poor, then you should strongly consider starting over from the beginning.

Producing a Final Draft of the Instrument

If you are fortunate and also worked very hard and got decent reliability, then you can make revisions and produce a final draft. Be sure to carefully consider the suggestions gleaned from the interviews, particularly those that refer to instructions. Once the final draft is complete, the pilot test should be repeated with another group. If the reliability holds or improves, the instrument is ready for use. The second pilot test may show lower reliability, however. Differences among the groups used for the pilot tests may be the cause for lower reliability, or the instrument may be unreliable. Continue revising and pilot testing until the reliability estimates are stable. Estimates within 5 percent of one another may be considered stable.

ADOPTING/ADAPTING AN INSTRUMENT

Why haven't we covered this topic before? It should be easier to use a test, scale or index that already exists than to make up a new one. That's right, it is, but the established instrument has to be appropriate for the people and the setting for measurement. Unfortunately, there isn't any magic formula to help decide whether the instrument is appropriate or not. To make an "educated guess" about the suitability of an instrument a series of steps can be followed. To illustrate how to decide whether to adopt or adapt an existing instrument or make up your own, let's go through the process step-by-step.

Sources of Instruments

The first issue for us to address in identifying instruments to adapt is where to begin looking. We can begin by consulting a broad-based index of literature like *INDEX MEDICUS*. This source categorizes an enormous amount of published research articles by subject and author. It may take awhile to explore your subject areas in the *INDEX MEDICUS*, but it is usually well worth the time spent. After writing down and tracking down the literature you found, you should be familiar with the instruments commonly used to do evaluations like yours as well as other methods used. This learning process is invaluable, and you should keep at it until you start seeing the same articles referenced repeatedly and the same methods used. When you reach this point you will have become familiar with the "state of the art" in evaluations like the one you are planning. At the same time you are reviewing literature, you should also be figuring out the most likely professional journals and other periodicals that are related to the area that you are evaluating. Once this is done, then a good thing to do is to spend time looking through those journals to see if you missed anything in your *INDEX MEDICUS* sources. Key words used for indexing are usually based on the title and methods, which may result in some good articles getting classified in a way that you wouldn't expect. As before, be on the lookout for articles that report evaluations similar to yours or, preferably (but rare), articles that publish reports on development of new instruments.

Assuming that you've found an article or articles that incorporate measurement that looks promising, the next step is to find out if the population that the other evaluators used is anything like yours. (A "promising" article is one in which the measurement that was used is clearly stated in terms of its type and reliability, deals with a subject very similar to yours, and used a similar population.) The article itself should give some information about this topic, but if it doesn't, don't be afraid to give the authors a call. Phone calls are sometimes better than letters, because when you call someone about their published research they are usually flattered and you might have the opportunity to get anecdotal comments on your own evaluation plans that are not normally included in letters. When you get information about the population that was used in the published research, then you are in a position to decide if you can use the instrument "as is" or whether you need to make adaptations for your population. (Remember that you need the permission of the author for any use of the instrument, usually in writing, and particularly if you need to make any changes.) Some established instruments are sold commercially, some are published in their entirety and are in the "public domain," and some are sensitive and you can't even buy them. The only way to find out whether you can use an instrument referred to in the literature is to ask.

It is important to understand that pilot testing of any instrument that you adopt or adapt is usually needed. Instruments that you use "as is" won't require extensive work, and the reliability should be known already. Adapted instruments, those that have been changed to suit your own needs, should be pilot tested just as any new instrument.

This chapter has outlined the basic procedures involved with development, testing, and adoption of scales and tests. The difference between instruments usually hinges on the motivation for their initial development. Tests are motivated by a need to estimate what an individual has learned; scales are usually motivated to assess feelings and thoughts.

READINGS

Karoly, P. (Ed.): *Measurement Strategies in Health Psychology.* New York, Wiley, 1985.
Lauffer, A.: *Assessment Tools for Practitioners, Managers and Trainers.* Beverly Hills, Sage, 1982.

McDowell, I., and Newell, C.: *Measuring Health: A Guide to Rating Scales and Questionnaires.* New York, Oxford, 1987.

Tuckman, B.W.: *Measuring Educational Outcomes: Fundamentals of Testing.* New York, Harcourt Brace Jovanovich, 1975.

USDHHS (PHS): *Index Medicus/National Library of Medicine.* Washington, D.C., 1985.

Chapter Five

MEASURING KNOWLEDGE

This chapter and the two that follow each address one of three specific targets of measurement: knowledge, attitudes and behavior. Since all three chapters deal with different applications of the same concepts, there is naturally some overlap of information. Even so, the three targets are distinct and the assumptions for measurement are fundamentally different, so separate treatment is needed.

THE NATURE OF THE TARGET OF MEASUREMENT

Before you can design a test to measure it, you need to be clear about what you mean by "knowledge." Knowledge is one of those words that can mean many things. Two of the many possible meanings might be: (1) recall of specific facts (we do this regularly in our system of education) or (2) the ability to apply specific facts to solving of a problem (we should do this more often). Depending on our meaning, then, measurement of knowledge can take on several different forms.

Knowledge is an abstraction. We can't see or touch knowledge, although we can often see the results of its application or maybe even sense its presence in some people. Because it is an abstraction and not a "real" thing, the measurement of knowledge puts us in a position where we have to come up with a different approach than we would use if we were measuring something that we could see and touch. For example, when we measure the size of a table top or the weight of a brick, we can see and touch what we want to measure. Our approach is straightforward and our methods familiar. We assign familiar units of measurement—feet, inches, pounds, or whatever—to the object to get our answer. The table top may be a rectangle measuring 4 feet by 5 feet; the brick may weigh 15 ounces. Because the units are standard, we can compare the weight or dimensions with other objects at will. With knowledge and other abstractions, there aren't any standard units like ounces and feet, or any standard methods of measurement, so we have to make up another way to measure what we want. We have to decide on a way to represent knowledge that will allow for development of a standard that we can use for comparison. However we decide to represent knowledge—the number of test items answered correctly, the number of steps in a procedure carried out correctly, etc.—the point is that our system is artificial. We made it up. We can change it to suit any need that we may have. Its validity and usability rest on the extent to which it has meaning that other people are willing to accept. It is very important to realize that fundamentally, all systems of measurement are made up for the purpose of assigning values to "things" both real and abstract, so that we can describe and compare what we measure with some degree of objectivity. Let's consider a simple example of this idea.

Suppose you have to choose among applicants for admission to a college. The information that you have at your fingertips to evaluate the applicants includes their grade point average from high school, scores on a standardized achievement test, record of attendance and letters of recommendation. Which of these would you choose for admitting students if your goal was to choose those with the best chance of doing well? Your choice depends on the assumptions that you decide to make about the measures. You could choose the grade point average, assuming that it probably represents an overall "average" of the students' ability to learn. As we said in an earlier chapter, though, the grade point average is only as accurate as the methods used to assign the letter grades which are the basis for the average. Suspicious of the grade point average, then, we could decide to look to the "standard" achievement test for guidance. These tests typically measure across a wide range of topic areas, break scores out in dimensions (verbal and quantitative, maybe), and compare each individual with everyone who took the test during some set period of time. This sounds pretty good, probably a better bet than the grade point average, but is it reasonable to expect a student to be able to demonstrate his/her potential for learning in college on one test taken in four hours? Suppose the student had a particularly good experience with the test on the day they took it and their score is a fluke? If this possibility makes us nervous, then we might decide to rely on attendance or letters of recommendation. These might seem farfetched compared to grades and test scores, but is it entirely unreasonable to imagine that the students that impressed their teachers the most and attended school the most also learned the most? Personal evaluation makes some sense, but we are trying to select those with the greatest potential for learning, and attendance and "impression" might not seem to address the future as much as the past. What makes the best sense, of course, is to use some combination of these measures, some combination that you believe summarizes the applicants' potential. You have to decide on indicators that will give the best measure of the abstract quality "potential for success." Knowledge Testing is Based on Two Main Assumptions:

(1) Asking questions can sample what an individual knows;

(2) A series of questions can summarize what an individual knows about a subject.

On a more practical level, the way we actually measure knowledge begins with two basic assumptions. First, we assume that it is possible to measure knowledge by asking questions that sample what the individual knows about a subject. Second, we assume that we can assemble our questions into a measurement instrument that can be scored to provide a meaningful summary that describes something about the individual's knowledge. Given these assumptions, wouldn't it make better sense to use performance of a task to demonstrate knowledge instead of a series of questions? Wouldn't we be better off if we saw how someone performed in solving a problem involving the knowledge we wanted to measure rather than relying on measurement of the knowledge as an abstraction? If you think about it, you'll realize that testing knowledge with paper-and-pencil tests relies on the basic belief that reactions to questions simulate reactions to the situations depicted by the questions. Don't get carried away with this idea, though, because decisions about the value of written questions as simulations are seldom clear cut. Sometimes this belief makes sense, but just as often it doesn't. You may give a test to see if students can count to four, for example, and if they can do it on the test it's probably reasonable to assume that they will be able to count four apples in the grocery store. If you ask questions about rules for traffic flow on the highway, on the other hand, it's probably not as reasonable to expect people to be able to apply the rules consistently, regardless of their knowledge. To measure knowledge well, we need to seriously consider the context of the subject we're trying to measure as well as keep the specific knowledge in clear focus.

DEVELOPING INSTRUMENTS
FOR MEASURING KNOWLEDGE

Our first task in developing methods for measurement is to clarify the meaning of measurement. A good way to structure thoughts about what we want to measure is to decide why we want to measure knowledge in the first place. What will the results be used for? If you want to use the results to decide which patients are least likely to take their medicines as directed, then what knowledge, if any, should be measured? What knowledge should be measured if you want to decide who should be promoted from the second to the third grade? What knowledge should we measure to decide which of two auto mechanics is better? If we know what we plan to do with the results, then we can decide what we mean by knowledge. Making this decision will give us a place to start. Once we've defined knowledge, we can move on to the next task of deciding just what sort of instrument we'll need for measurement. (This process is always much easier if you have objectives to guide you, by the way.)

Instrument Design

Once the basic decision is made about what knowledge is to be measured, the next step is to begin design of the instrument. A good way to begin is to imagine what you would want to see in looking at the results from people taking the test. How much did they know about the subject? How much did they not know? What specifically did they know and not know? These questions are very basic, and sometimes difficult to answer, but they form the foundation for any knowledge test. The answers to the questions about what you want to learn from the results of the test will lead to more in-depth thinking about the objectives for the test.

Using Objectives

Objectives, in some form, are needed if a good knowledge test is to be developed. Developing objectives can be irritating but it is good discipline because it forces you to slow down and really think about what you are trying to measure, as well as what the program is trying to accomplish. Once you have a complete set of objectives, the next task is to order them in terms of **priority** and **sequence**. Priority means putting the most important objectives at the head of the list and the least important near the bottom. The place on the list implies the emphasis that you plan to give to measuring the objective. Sequence means some ordering, within priority, that makes sense in terms of how the material is presented or how people ordinarily think about the subject. For example, if we taught a unit to a men's group about preventing heart disease, our objectives might include topics like anatomy and physiology of the circulatory system, signs and symptoms of cardiovascular disease, first aid for heart attack, heart disease and health behavior, and ways to change behavior to prevent heart disease. We might prioritize the objectives from these topics, putting those dealing with health behavior and behavior change near the top of the list, first aid for heart attack and recognition of signs and symptoms next, and the anatomy and physiology last. Within these categories for objectives, we might decide on a sequencing for the objectives, like "the heart is a pump" followed by "blood pressure is based on the contractions of the heart" for anatomy and physiology, based on the way we planned to present the information. Taking the time to think through our objectives in this way will help us to make several key decisions about the knowledge test.

Deciding on Item Type

Once the objectives are developed, prioritized and ordered, the next task is to decide on the types of items to use. We can use several different types to measure knowledge. Essay, short answer, multiple choice, true-false, matching and completion are probably the most popular types of items. Deciding on which types to use is based on what you want to learn from the results. If you want to measure basic processes like recognition of key words, recall of specific facts, or ability to make basic connections, then essay and short-answer types of items are NOT a good choice. Essay and short-answer items are most useful for measuring how well the individual expresses her/himself and puts information together (synthesis). Objective-type items (multiple choice, for example) are better for measuring recognition and recall. Another consideration in choosing item types is the amount of objectivity and efficiency needed in scoring the test. Items where the individual indicates the answer simply by marking a choice can be scored very quickly and, since the scorer does not have to make any judgment, objectivity is not really an issue. Objectivity can become an issue when an answer has to be interpreted, as in essay and short-answer items. On the other hand, the evaluation of a person's understanding of the information might require more expression than simply indicating the choice of an answer, and might have to be subjective in some cases. You have to decide on the types of items to include based on the specific goals of measuring knowledge in the first place, the characteristics of the people who will be taking the test, the environmental conditions (the amount of time available, facilities, etc.), and the nature of the information needed.

Developing Items

When the types of items to be used have been selected, the items themselves need to be developed. It's a good practice to begin by developing the essence of the items in the form of statements, based on the objectives. For example, the objective mentioned earlier, "blood pressure is based on the contractions of the heart," could also be a statement. This statement could be a true-false item as is, or easily modified to serve as a stem, the basic statement for an objective item, for a multiple-choice item. For example, "blood pressure is at its greatest when the heart _____" (which could also serve as a completion item). The foils are the possible answers for objective multiple-choice type items. The choice of foils is important, because the difficulty of the item often depends on how much sense each makes in answering the question. If we used "contracts," "relaxes," "stops," and "starts," then the only question to be answered would be deciding on which of the first two to choose; "stops" and "starts" are pretty farfetched and would only be chosen by people who were confused or totally uninformed.

When a draft of the items is completed, the directions should be developed and the test assembled. The directions need to be crystal clear. If different types of items are used, they shouldn't be mixed in the test unless absolutely necessary. Arranging tests so that items are together by type reduces the chance for confusion due to changing the method for answering. It is also a good practice to arrange items so that a few of the easier ones come first in the test. Having initial success is often helpful in building confidence in the test taker and promotes better performance. A useful principle to keep in mind is anything that interferes with or distracts the test taker is likely to produce unsystematic error. Remember, unsystematic error reduce reliability.

When complete, the test needs to be pilot tested. Using people who are as similar to those you will be measuring as possible, go through a "dry run" with the instrument. Include all the procedures for administration that you plan to use in collecting the evaluation data, including scoring and any interpretation. It's a good idea to interview a few of the people who take the test for you to find out if there are any areas of confusion that aren't apparent. The results of scoring the test allow you to conduct an "item analysis," an important "test" of your test.

EXAMPLES OF KNOWLEDGE TEST ITEM TYPES

Multiple Choice:

Circle the type of test item that is best suited for measuring recall and recognition.

a. essay

b. short answer

c. multiple choice

d. none of the above

True-False:

Knowledge can only be measured using objective-type test items.

a. True

b. False

Matching:

Match the item types on the left with the phrases on the right.

__ Completion   a. Recall and Recognition

__ True-False   b. Recall, written expression

__ Short Answer   c. Ability to integrate information

__ Multiple Choice   d. Written expression

Completion:

In beginning to organize a knowledge test, one of the first steps is to organize objectives by _____ and sequence.

Short-Answer:

Briefly describe the uses of objective-type items in knowledge testing.

Essay:

Justify the use of objective, short-answer and essay type items in the measurement of knowledge. What, if any, unique information is contributed by each item type?

ITEM ANALYSIS

Once you have collected pilot data, it can be used to estimate the reliability and validity of the test in a different way than presented in Chapter Three. (The technical aspects are presented in the Appendix to this chapter.) Item analysis is an analytic procedure for examining how much each item contributes to the test as a whole. To have a good test, we need to have a set of items that can be answered by those who have the knowledge that we want to measure. At the same time, we want those who do not have the knowledge not to be able to answer the questions as well as those individuals with more knowledge. If knowledgeable people aren't able to answer the questions, then naturally our test isn't valid. Likewise, our test is equally invalid if people manage to get the right answers even though they don't have the knowledge. The results of item analysis are specific and point to troublesome items in the test. These items need to be corrected and, if there are a sizable number needing corrections, the test pilot tested again.

In this chapter we have presented the basic ideas that underlie measuring knowledge. The most basic challenge we face in measuring knowledge is trying to figure out what we want to measure, what we mean by "knowledge," in other words. The way we design measurement instruments depends on what we want to learn about those we measure as well as what we want to be able to do with the results.

READINGS

Morris, L.L., and Fitz-Gibbon, C.T.: *How to Measure Achievement.* Beverly Hills, Sage, 1978.
Schoer, L.A.: *Test Construction: A Programmed Guide.* Boston, Allyn & Bacon, 1970.

TECHNICAL APPENDIX

ITEM ANALYSIS

Item analysis is a technique that can be used to evaluate how the pattern of the answers given to individual items on a test contribute to the total scores obtained. In using item analysis to assess an instrument, we assume that the greater the number of items that the individual answers correctly, the greater their knowledge. In making this assumption, we also assume that the worth of the instrument is determined by the worth of each item in distinguishing between those who have knowledge and those who do not. Item analysis produces two useful results: an assessment of the contribution of each item to the total score, and information that can be used to develop better items that will improve the test. Item analysis produces two pieces of information about each item on the instrument: difficulty and discrimination. Item difficulty is a straightforward idea and basically reflects the number of people completing the instrument who answered the item correctly. Discrimination is somewhat more complicated than difficulty. An item that is a "good discriminator" is one that was answered correctly by those with high scores on the instrument, and incorrectly by those with low scores. We'll use an example to illustrate the details.

Suppose we developed a knowledge test for patients in a cardiac rehabilitation program. The program teaches the patients about heart disease, exercise, diet, and stress control, in addition to providing supervised exercise. Our knowledge test consists of twenty multiple-choice items. Item analysis is a four-step process. We begin by scoring the tests and arranging them in order from highest to lowest. For this example, assume that 25 people took the test.

Step One: Score the Tests and Arrange the Scores in Order

The array of scores from our test looks like this:

20, 18, 18, 17, 17, 17, 15, 15, 15, 13, 13, 13, 13, 13, 13, 13, 12, 12, 12, 11, 10, 10, 10, 9, 9

Next, we need to divide the list of test scores into thirds. (Some recommend fourths; the point is to have as many scores as possible in two "extreme" groups.) Since there is an uneven number of scores, we'll take the top and bottom eight scores to use for the analysis and ignore the middle nine. It's always best to have an even number of scores in the groups.

Step Two: Identify the Top and Bottom Thirds (or Fourths) of the Scores for Use in the Analysis. Separate out the test answer sheets that correspond with the scores selected.

Top Third	Bottom Third
20	12
18	12
18	11
17	10
17	10
17	10
15	9
15	9

The next step is to construct an item analysis chart and complete the columns for each item. (The term "success" refers to the number of people who answered the item correctly.) A sample table with several of the items from our test is shown below.

Step Three: Complete the Item Analysis Chart

ITEM ANALYSIS CHART

item number	success of upper group	success of lower group	index of discrimination $(U - L)$	level of difficulty $(U + L)$
1	6	4	2	10
2	8	7	1	15
4	7	7	0	14
5	5	6	−1	11
10	7	7	0	14
12	8	4	4	12
13	6	8	−2	14
18	8	7	1	15

Success: the number correctly answering a particular item.

Step Four: Interpret the Information on the Item Analysis Chart

Using the item analysis chart, you can interpret the discrimination and difficulty of each item. An item that is a "good discriminator" is one that distinguishes between the upper and lower groups and also favors the upper group. To interpret the discrimination indices, we can use the following rules. For any discrimination index value D, where N is the number of items in the test:

> If D is › N/2, then the item is a "good" discriminator.
> If N/2 › D › N/5, then the item is a "fair" discriminator.
> If D › N/5, then the item is a "poor" discriminator.
> If D = 0, then the item does not discriminate at all.
> If D = 0, then the item is a "negative discriminator."*

Interpretation of the level of difficulty is easier than discrimination. Guidelines for interpretation are as follows. Of those completing the test in both upper and lower groups:

> If › 70% answer correctly, the item is "easy."
> If 30%–70% answer correctly, the item is "moderate."
> If ‹ 30% answer correctly, the item is "difficult."

Using the guidelines shown above for discrimination and difficulty, the results of our test turned out as follows:

Item number	Discrimination†	Difficulty‡
1	1-P	10-M
2	1-P	15-M
4	0-N	14-M
5	− 1-Neg	11-M
10	0-N	14-M
12	4-F	12-M
13	− 2-Neg	14-M
18	0-N	14-M

The results of the item analysis seem to show that our test is not going to discriminate between those patients who learned and those who didn't. The primary reason for this is that the items do not include a wide enough range of difficulty. There are also two negative discriminators.

---

*Items are negative discriminators when there are more correct answers among those in the lower group than the upper group.

†For discrimination: let P = poor, F = fair, N = none, and NEG = negative.

‡For difficulty: let D = difficult, M = moderate, and E = easy.

Based on the results of the item analysis, we would want to change items 5 and 13 because they are negative discriminators. It is likely that these items are either poorly worded or otherwise confusing so that the correct answers are more likely to come from guessing than knowledge. The low difficulty and poor discrimination of items 2 and 4 fit with our aim of having easy items early in the test. We won't change them. The rest of the items need to be re-examined and their level of difficulty upgraded. A second pilot test and item analysis should also be done with the new version of the test.

READINGS

Lien, Arnold J.: *Measurement and Evaluation of Learning,* 3rd ed. Dubuque, Brown, 1976.

Chapter Six

MEASURING ATTITUDES

This chapter is devoted to discussion of the measurement of attitudes. Like the previous chapter on measurement of knowledge, this chapter will be organized to present the basic idea first followed by specific methods that can be used for measurement.

ATTITUDES AS TARGETS OF MEASUREMENT

Attitudes are essentially opinions. Most health educators have long been concerned with influencing attitudes because it is widely believed that attitudes are related to behaviors, and behavior change is a basic goal of health education and health promotion. The nature of this connection is not always clear, however. In some cases it appears that attitudes may predict behaviors, while in others, attitudes seem to be reflected in behaviors. Understanding attitudes is an important part of understanding behavior. Measuring attitudes with accuracy is a formidable challenge, however.

Opinions (attitudes) are usually related to specific topics or issues. Almost by default, we use opinions to summarize our feelings. Let's consider as an example the issue of smoking. The predominant medical evidence points to a conclusion that smoking is dangerous, primarily because it is so closely associated with so many serious diseases. Based on this conclusion, most physicians agree that smoking is a habit that should be stopped and preferably never started. The negative attitude of health professionals toward smoking is clear. The attitude toward smoking is translated into physician behavior that discourages smoking among physicians and their patients. In this case, the attitude would be expected to predict the behavior.

While the relationship between attitude and behavior may be unclear at times and we may not be able to confidently predict one from another, there is usually a "direction" to this relationship. If we were to measure a physician's attitudes and found that she felt that smoking was dangerous, then we would probably be safe in assuming that she would encourage her patients not to smoke. On the other hand, if she didn't feel that smoking was dangerous, it is less likely that she would encourage her patients to stop.

In many instances, attitudes are related to past learning. The learning may be in the form of modeled behavior, as from a parent, or in the form of personal experience. The past learning genesis of attitudes forms an important part of the measurement process: the context. The context, the situations that are identified with attitudes and their development, provides information that may be crucial to interpretation. For example, attitudes toward smoking are often based on experience. People with relatives who have suffered from smoking-related illnesses may have an understandably hostile attitude toward smokers, tobacco companies and others who advocate smoking. On the other hand, those who have been around smokers and who have experienced no ill effects may be skeptical of claims of the dangers associated with smoking. Information that contradicts these attitudes may be totally ineffective in producing change, regardless of its validity. An important concept to keep in mind regarding attitudes is that nearly all people are motivated to believe that their point of view is correct. They aren't necessarily motivated to be correct so much as they are to believe that they are correct. To preserve this notion, an individual may adopt or distort information to make it fit with his/her preconceived attitude about the issue in question.

To summarize our discussion thus far, attitudes are a distinct entity to measure. Measuring attitudes requires a different conceptual framework from measuring knowledge. Attitudes are more inferred than demonstrated. They are abstract qualities that we cannot measure directly. Attitudes are often inconsistent and can vary widely within the same individual. Behavior that we use to infer attitudes may be dependent on the context and not representative of the person's usual behavior. As the context changes, the attitude may also change. Finally, attitudes are operationally defined. There are no universally accepted guidelines to be used.

APPROACHES TO ATTITUDE MEASUREMENT

Capturing attitudes and assigning them value in some type of numerical system is quite different from measuring knowledge. When we measure knowledge we often have objectives to work from. Objectives serve to divide what we are trying to measure into separate parts that can be combined into a whole. Attitudes are not necessarily divisible into component parts. Instead, we must consider attitudes as abstract constructs in terms of a varying contextual framework. To illustrate, knowledge of danger from smoking may be decomposed into parts such as "effects of cyanide," "effects of particulate matter," etc. Attitudes toward smoking cannot easily be decomposed into parts that correspond to areas of knowledge that can be verified. Instead, it makes more sense to think about attitudes changing slightly depending on the context. To make matters even more complex, attitudes can appear to be quite different depending on an individual's frame of mind at the time. For example, smokers' attitudes toward their habit often change when they get sick and have trouble breathing. Smoking becomes less enjoyable as breathing gets more difficult, and negative attitudes toward the habit usually get stronger. Unfortunately, when the infection clears and breathing becomes easier, the attitudes toward smoking that were so strongly negative become less so, and resolve to quit smoking dissipates.

Most evaluations require numerical descriptions for attitudes. Given their nature, assigning numbers to descriptions of attitudes is a subjective matter. Consider the following analogy. Imagine measuring heights of a group of children. You can easily assign numerical values to their heights using feet, inches, feet and inches, centimeters, millimeters, etc. Another way to approach the problem, though, would be to find the tallest, shortest, or most average child, and use that child's height as a standard to describe the heights of all the other children. The disadvantage of the latter method is that you have to know how tall the "standard child" is to be able to figure out how tall the rest of the kids are. On the other hand, you don't have to translate numbers into a visual representation of "height" as you would if the former (numerical) method was used. Describing the children's heights in terms of a "standard height of children of a specific age" is analogous to the way we have to measure attitudes. Since we don't have universally accepted standards for defining attitudes, we have to describe the attitudes of individuals as they compare to attitudes that we can communicate. At Christmastime, for example, we all know what we mean by being a "scrooge." A scrooge is someone with a sour attitude about Christmas. The attitude is not something that we can measure like height or weight, but we don't have any trouble naming it when we see it because it stands out as different from the "jolly" attitude we expect at that time of year. Acting like a scrooge at

Christmas demonstrates a definite attitude. The point is that we are able to identify and name the attitude because of a standard that we have decided to use.

Actually measuring attitudes for the purpose of evaluation requires a more "objective" system than comparisons based on informal systems like the "scrooge index." We have to decide on a means of describing the attitudes in question using a systematic, if not objective, approach.

The "scrooge index" example also illustrates the importance of culture and cultural sensitivity in attitude measurement. In this context, cultural sensitivity is the inclusion of relevant elements of the culture of the target population in planning and implementing attitude measurement. It is very important that elements of the culture that relate to attitudes be identified during the planning for attitude measurement and that the instruments developed reflect an awareness of culture. Language, terminology, sex-role expectations and life-style are areas where cultural differences often influence attitudes. For example, many Native American tribes avoid getting information by asking direct questions. Direct questions are considered intrusive and rude. Many tribes are also matriarchal and matrilineal. Attitude measurement of such populations would not be successful, and could be offensive, if these cultural features were ignored. Taking care to understand cultural features that may relate to the area being measured is an important step in developing instruments. Asking people who are part of the culture to participate in pilot testing of early versions of the instrument is invaluable in making sure that measurement will proceed smoothly.

METHODS FOR MEASURING ATTITUDES

We will present three basic approaches to measuring attitudes in this chapter: equal-interval, summated ratings, and semantic differential. Remember that even though these methods differ quite a bit, they are intended to do the same thing: measure and describe attitudes. Because attitudes are essentially opinions, each of the methods used to measure attitudes seeks to do so by assessing opinions using paper-and-pencil methods. Each of the attitude measurement methods presented in this chapter is based on the same concept, namely, that an attitude can be detected through reactions to written terms or statements. For example, the reaction of a person reading the statement, "Behavior doesn't matter, genetics control health," provides information about their attitude toward the role of behavior in protecting health. This single statement doesn't reveal everything about their attitude of course, but if we were to add more statements we could collect more and more information about the person's attitude. Equal-interval, summated ratings and semantic differential are three techniques for using sets of terms or statements to elicit reactions that reflect attitudes.

Equal-Interval Measurement

Equal-interval scales, also known as "Thurstone" scales after L.L. Thurstone their inventor, require considerable effort to develop but are valuable because of relatively easy administration and scoring. The basic idea behind these scales is that attitudes about issues exist in gradations on an (imaginary) continuum from positive to negative and, therefore, the attitude of one person can be described according to its place on the continuum.

Item Development

The first step in developing the continuum of attitudes is to clearly describe the attitude in question. It is helpful to come up with a very short phrase or even one word that will communicate the attitude. For example, the phrases "birth control" and "family planning" might be used to communicate attitudes toward using contraception to limit family size, prevent conception in general, or provide stress-free sexual relations. The next step in constructing an equal-interval scale is to develop a large number (at least 50) of statements that describe various aspects of the attitude and its components. The statements should be opinions and not facts. They should include positive, negative and neutral opinions. "Using birth control is the best thing a person could ever do"; "no one should ever use birth control"; and "using birth control is up to the individual" are typical statements of opinions related to birth control.

Scale Development

When the statements have been developed, the next step is to submit them to at least three "expert" judges who will rank them in terms of the attitude conveyed. The judges should be "experts" in terms of being familiar with common attitudes like the ones you want to measure. The judges should be instructed to rank the statements into categories ranging from "most positive" to "neutral" to "most negative." When the judges have ranked the statements, the rankings of all the judges are summarized to come up with an "average" ranking for each statement. The statements that generated the clearest agreement among the judges' rankings are best for use in the attitude scale. You need to select at least 25 items that represent the range of the continuum according to their "average" ranking, from positive to negative, in roughly equal proportions. If the judges' rankings don't allow you to select enough items to fulfill the requirements for the scale, then you'll need to develop more items and ask the judges to rank them. Arrange the items in order from most positive to most negative, using the "average" rankings of the judges. The most positive statement will be the first item of your scale, the most negative statement the last.

Scoring

Equal-interval scales traditionally include an odd number of statements, with the "middle" statement being neutral. Statements on either side of the middle get progressively more opinionated, positively on one side and negatively on the other. Each statement on the scale is assigned a value, for the purpose of scoring. The middle neutral statement is assigned the value of 0.0. The assigned values increase by 0.2, positive and negative, to the first and last statements on the scale. If 25 statements are used, the most positive statement, usually the first statement in the scale, would be assigned the value of $+5.0$ and the last statement in the scale, the most negative attitude, -5.0.

When the items are assembled and the values assigned, the directions need to be developed. The directions for completing an equal-interval scale are simple. All the individual has to do is indicate which items she/he agrees with in terms of the subject of the scale. For example, "With regard to the issue of using birth control, please circle the numbers of the statements you agree with." Scoring is also easy for equal-interval scales. The score of the individual is the median (middle value) of the values of the statements chosen.

Interpreting Results from Thurstone Attitude Scales

Interpretation of scores from attitude scales deserves careful discussion. First, we need to ask what type of number (scale of measurement) we get from scoring equal-interval attitude scales. It isn't really an interval scale number at all, but an indicator of attitude relative to a neutral attitude. The score indicates where the person ranks on the continuum from positive to negative. Although we assigned values, we don't have any idea of the "attitude" distance between the statements. We certainly can't be sure that it is equal, so the scale of measurement has to be ordinal. With ordinal measurement we can't say that two people with scores of 3.4 and 4.0 differ in attitude by 0.6; all we can say is that one is more positive than the other. With this in mind, we can interpret the attitude scale scores as "positive," "strongly positive," "neutral" and so on, but it wouldn't make any sense to report the numerical scores as interval or ratio scale numbers. Likewise, we have to be careful in describing the attitude of a group and avoid using terms like "average." "Strongly positive," "negative," and other qualitative descriptions are appropriate, however.

The validity of equal-interval scales is based on the extent to which the statements adequately cover the continuum of opinion about the subject. The use of "expert" judges bolsters the claim of "content validity." The reliability of these scales can be determined most readily by the test-retest method. Figure 6-1 shows an equal-interval Attitude scale.

Summated Ratings

The phrase "summated ratings" means that the score from this type of attitude measurement is the sum of ratings from individual items. This approach is totally different from the equal-interval method. There is no underlying continuum of the attitude that we are trying to use to judge individual attitudes, nor is there any assumption that we can divide the attitude into gradations. The summated ratings approach has more flexibility than the equal-interval method and allows for easier introduction of context into the measurement process. Context is often very important to measuring attitudes, because many attitudes are specific to particular people, places, events, or things. Lots of people like ice cream, for example, but don't think of eating it during the cold months of the year. Summated rating scales have a form that is probably very familiar to you. The form is sometimes known as a "Likert" format, after its originator. Figure 6-2 shows summated ratings attitude scale items.

As you can see, unlike the equal-interval format, the person expressing their attitude has more freedom of expression than with an equal-interval approach. Likewise, the scale developer has more freedom to vary the context and measure the attitude in varying contexts.

This scale was designed to assess **attitudes toward smoking.** The instructions are to circle the numbers next to each statement that you agree with. The scoring values shown on the left are not included on the attitude scale.

Scoring
Value

−2.4	1. Smoking is the worst thing a person could ever do.
−2.2	2. Smoking is self destructive.
−2.0	3. Smoking is a sign of a poor self concept.
−1.8	4. Smoking shows how weak people can be.
−1.6	5. Smoking is a sign that a person needs a crutch.
−1.4	6. Smoking is not a good idea.
−1.2	7. Smoking is a bad habit.
0.0	8. Smoking is neither good or bad.
1.2	9. Smoking is a good habit.
1.4	10. Smoking is okay.
1.6	11. Smoking is a sign of independence.
1.8	12. Smoking shows that people can make their own decisions.
2.0	13. Smoking shows self confidence.
2.2	14. Smoking is harmless.
2.4	15. Smoking is the best thing a person could ever do.

A 25-year-old who smokes at least 1 pack of cigarettes each day completed the attitude scale. He circled items 5, 10, 11 and 12, which correspond to values of −1.6, 1.4, 1.6 and 1.8. Negative values correspond to negative attitudes toward smoking and positive values favor smoking. The attitude score of the 25-year-old smoker is a 1.5, midway between 1.4 and 1.6, the two middle values he circled. We might describe his attitude toward smoking as "slightly positive."

Note: If an odd number of items are circled, the score is the value of the middle item circled.

Figure 6-1. An example of an Equal-Interval Attitude Scale.

Development

The items for summated ratings are created out of the imagination of the developer of the scale. Since context is important, items can be developed that vary the context of opinion about the subject, and expert judges can be used to review the items. The judges don't formally rank the items but can be used to give feedback about coverage of the range and intensity of feelings about the issue. An issue that sometimes arises is the use of a neutral or undecided response to the items. Some feel that there should be seven responses possible; strongly agree, moderately agree, agree, undecided, disagree, moderately disagree and strongly disagree. Others believe that five possible responses are adequate, usually eliminating the "moderately" category. Another school of thought is that the neutral (undecided) response shouldn't be used because many people tend to hide their true opinions by choosing them repeatedly.

The items shown below could be used in measuring attitudes toward smoking. The instructions for completing the scale are indicate your opinion about each item by checking the term or statement that best expresses your opinion.

1. Smoking is self destructive.

   ___ strongly agree   ___ agree   ___ undecided   ___ disagree   ___ strongly disagree

2. Smoking is a sign of a poor self concept.

   ___ strongly agree   ___ agree   ___ undecided   ___ disagree   ___ strongly disagree

3. Smoking is a sign of independence.

   ___ strongly agree   ___ agree   ___ undecided   ___ disagree   ___ strongly disagree

4. Smoking shows how weak people can be.

   ___ strongly agree   ___ agree   ___ undecided   ___ disagree   ___ strongly disagree

5. Smoking is harmless.

   ___ strongly agree   ___ agree   ___ undecided   ___ disagree   ___ strongly disagree

6. Smoking is a sign that a person needs a crutch.

   ___ strongly agree   ___ agree   ___ undecided   ___ disagree   ___ strongly disagree

7. Smoking shows that people can make their own decisions.

   ___ strongly agree   ___ agree   ___ undecided   ___ disagree   ___ strongly disagree

For Scoring, values are given to each response category as follows:

2	1	0	-1	-2
strongly agree	agree	undecided	disagree	strongly disagree

The total score is the sum of the values for each item.

Figure 6-2. Summated Ratings Scale Iems (Likert format).

Scales that don't have an undecided or neutral response possibility are sometimes called "forced choice." You need to decide how best to structure your scale based on the attitude you want to measure and the people that will be completing the scale.

Administration and Scoring

The administration and scoring of summated ratings scales are straight-forward. The directions are simple, instructing the person to check the one blank for each item that best describes his/her opinion about the statement. To score the instrument, the traditional procedure is to assign values to the choices for each item and simply add them up to get a total score. The one wrinkle in the scoring system is that for instruments with an "undecided" category, it is best to give that choice a value of 0, agree $+1$, strongly agree $+2$, disagree -1, and strongly disagree -2. The values assigned for "forced-choice" formats can be more flexible: $+1$ for strongly disagree, $+2$ for disagree, and on up to $+4$ for strongly agree.

Interpretation of Results from Summated Ratings Scales

The point behind the scoring systems is to give a total score that will summarize the attitude. If one person has a positive attitude, indicated by agreeing with most of the items, then you want his/her score to be distinct from another person with the opposite attitude. For instruments that include "undecided", the 0 will reduce their score dramatically if they choose undecided for very many items. Those with positive attitudes will have scores with a positive sign; those with negative attitudes will have negative scores. These scoring systems are not sacred by any means, and you may experiment and develop a system that works better for your needs. Regardless of the way you decide to score the instrument, the system needs to be included in the report of the results. As we mentioned before, the numerical scores from attitude scales are not used themselves. The way the scores were derived is important, though, because the statements we make about attitudes reflect the scores.

Semantic Differential Scales

The third method of attitude measurement that we will present is based on a concept that is distinct from both summated ratings and equal-interval scales. The semantic differential, sometimes called "adjective pairs," is based on the idea that the way an individual reacts to an issue, and makes her/his attitude apparent, can be measured by the way he/she favors adjectives that describe various aspects of the issue in question. In the contrived example shown below, the individual's attitude toward ice cream can be measured by having them put an "X" between each pair of adjectives.

The original developers of the semantic differential technique invested considerable time and effort in establishing the procedures. The reference by Osgood, Suci, and Tannenbaum, listed at the end of this chapter, should be consulted for an in-depth explanation of this method. As you might imagine, there is a certain type of cleverness that goes into developing the semantic differential that is different from that needed for the other types of attitude measures (see Figure 6-3). The choice of adjective pairs can lead the individual into whatever aspects of the issue that you want to explore. Like the summated ratings procedure, the semantic differential allows expression about the issue and, if you are clever, exploration of the context of attitudes.

Development

Development of semantic differential scales rests on selection of the adjectives primarily, in addition to identification and development of phrases that effectively communicate aspects of the attitude that you want to measure. The reference that we mentioned earlier by Osgood, Suci, and Tannenbaum includes a sizable list of adjectives that you may want to choose from in developing a semantic differential, or you can develop your own. The usual practice is to develop at least four or five phrases to communicate the attitude, like the phrase "ice cream" in the example, and use the same adjective pairs with each. You should plan on at least 12 adjective pairs for each phrase used.

Administration and Scoring

Clear directions are very important for semantic differentials. Always include an example showing how the person should respond as part of the directions. Scoring of semantic differential instruments uses the same conceptual basis as summated ratings. By convention, a value of 0 is assigned to the middle choice. The choices in the direction of the positive adjective are assigned values of $+1$, $+2$ and $+3$; the choices toward the negative adjective -1, -2 and -3. The total score is obtained by adding up the values from each item.

The instructions for completing semantic differential scales are to indicate your opinion in terms of the pairs of words (adjectives) provided. For example, if you like eating ice cream, you might check the pairs as shown below.

Ice Cream

Good   _XX_ ____ ____ ____ ____ ____ ____   Awful

Exercise

Tiring   ____ ____ ____ ____ ____ ____ ____   Refreshing

Rewarding   ____ ____ ____ ____ ____ ____ ____   Punishing

Easy   ____ ____ ____ ____ ____ ____ ____   Difficult

Unpleasant   ____ ____ ____ ____ ____ ____ ____   Enjoyable

Building   ____ ____ ____ ____ ____ ____ ____   Destructive

Frustrating   ____ ____ ____ ____ ____ ____ ____   Stimulating

Expensive   ____ ____ ____ ____ ____ ____ ____   Affordable

Scoring for the semantic differential is carried out by assigning values to each blank, taking care to reverse the order when the positive and negative adjectives are reversed. See the example shown below.

| Building | 3 | 2 | 1 | 0 | -1 | -2 | -3 | Destructive |
| Frustrating | -3 | -2 | -1 | 0 | 1 | 2 | 3 | Stimulating |

The total score on the attitude scale is the sum of the values of the blanks checked for each adjective pair.

Figure 6-3. Semantic Differential Attitude Scale Items.

Interpretation of Results from Semantic Differential Scales

Pilot testing with semantic differentials is crucial, since effective communication is so important. You should interview several people who completed the pilot instrument to learn how well they understood your point. Validity of semantic differentials can be demonstrated by discriminant processes, or multitrait-multimethod; reliability by test-retest, or internal consistency.

GENERAL GUIDELINES FOR DEVELOPING ATTITUDE SCALES

There are several cautions that you should remember in developing and using attitude scales. Remember that attitudes are not so much "measured" by the scales as they are "inferred." Attitudes are also unstable sometimes and dependent to a large extent on the context. To get the best results, always pilot test the scales using individuals or groups with "known" attitudes toward the issue in question. Look for response set in the completed scales, where people obviously didn't think about each item, but marked the same way all the time. (Keep them on their toes, so to speak, by changing the response format. Every third or fourth item on summated ratings and semantic differentials should have the order of choices reversed.)

Some specific guidelines to keep in mind for all attitude scales are as follows:

1. Avoid factual statements. Remember that you are trying to find out how the person feels about the issue. Factual questions usually get you answers about knowledge, not attitudes.
2. Avoid referring to the past. Your statements should be written to refer to the present or future, where attitudes are current or will be developed.
3. Avoid multiple interpretations. This is easier said than done, but items that are written so that there is more than one interpretation cannot be answered or scored easily. The best attitude measurement scales have items that are clear and unambiguous.
4. Avoid irrelevant items. Each item should be written to contribute to inferring individual attitudes. Items that nearly everyone agrees or disagrees with don't help in distinguishing attitudes. They may be useful for examples, though.
5. Cover the entire range of attitudes toward an issue. If your scale is obviously weighted toward the positive or negative, then it is likely that the person will respond more to the bias in the scale than the items themselves.
6. Avoid items that include more than one thought. Items with "or" or "and" usually convey more than one thought and are commonly open to more than one interpretation. Make separate items from those with multiple thoughts.
7. Avoid "giveaway" language. Terms such as "always," "all," and

so on usually make items appear to be conveying extreme attitudes. Use such terms sparingly.

8. Avoid double negatives. Use simple and clear language.

READINGS

Lien, A.J.: *Measurement and Evaluation of Learning,* 3rd ed. Dubuque, Brown, 1976.

Osgood, C.E., Suci, G.J., and Tannenbaum, P.H.: *The Measurement of Meaning.* Urbana, University of Illinois Press, 1957.

Tuckman, B.W.: *Measuring Educational Outcomes: Fundamentals of Testing.* New York, Harcourt Brace Jovanovich, 1975.

Vincent, R.J.: New scale for measuring attitudes. *School Health Review,* 5(2), 19, 1974.

Chapter Seven

MEASURING HEALTH BEHAVIOR

This is the last of three chapters that deal with specific targets of measurement: knowledge, attitude and behavior. This chapter is distinct from the two previous, in that while the chapters on knowledge and attitude measurement were focused on measuring abstractions, behaviors are real. In some ways it is easier to measure abstract things like attitudes and knowledge, because we don't have to be directly concerned with behavior. In fact, it is common to measure knowledge and attitude, primarily because we can't measure behavior. Still, in most cases the basic motivation for measurement is that we want to be able to describe, or at least document, behavior. After all, whether we teach a lesson, give advice on eating a low-salt diet, or prescribe a medicine, the ultimate goal is to improve the lives of the people taught by helping them to change their behaviors. In measuring knowledge or attitudes we might learn what the people absorbed from our teaching or how they felt about the new information, but we won't learn whether they use any of the information. Measuring behavior allows us to try to answer this question.

BEHAVIOR AS A TARGET OF MEASUREMENT

Behaviors occur in context. That is, other actors in the scenes of our lives, other people and events, all play a part in our behavior. When we attempt to measure behavior of an individual, it is a challenging prospect in the sense that it is difficult for us to measure the behavior as well as the context. Consider an example. Suppose you are in a grocery store and you see a parent scolding their child. If you just walked into the store and came upon this scene, then your immediate reaction can only be based on what you see. Perhaps you are upset by what you see; perhaps you feel that the parent should be behaving differently. But consider the situation from another point of view. Suppose that you didn't just walk in; rather, you were waiting in line with the parent and her child for several minutes. In that case you would have a different impression of the parent's behavior because you would have a context in which to put the parent's behavior. Now suppose that we were bold enough to think that we could measure "discipline skills" in parents of small children by merely observing their behavior. If we didn't know the context in which the behaviors occurred, we would be missing a vital part of our behavioral observation. Because of the complexity of the context, measurement of behavior can be far more complicated than measurement of knowledge or attitudes.

Would it make a difference in measuring behavior if the parent was a male or female? What about the sex of the child? Would the ages of the parent and child matter? What about the race or ethnic group (culture) of the parent and child? Depending on who is observing the parent and child interactions, factors such as sex, age and culture (based on appearance or language) may play significant roles in measurement. In some cultures, loud voices and animated gestures may be routine parts of parent-child interactions while in other cultures such behaviors may only occur rarely. The sex and age of the parent and child may also figure heavily in observations of behavior. The influence of culture and personal characteristics (sex and age) of the subjects of measurement of behaviors, as well as those doing the measurement, is not clearly defined. Nevertheless, cultural and personal factors are important components of the measurement of health behaviors.

Defining Behavior

Perhaps the most basic thing to remember about measuring behavior (and the thing that distinguishes it from knowledge and attitudes) is that behavior has to be rigidly defined. We need to be careful here, because it is not necessary to be as dogmatic as this may appear. When we measure behavior we are focusing on the observable, or the unmistakable signs of the observable. This is a different conceptual approach from knowledge and attitude measurement, in the sense that when we measure behavior we are only concerned with recording what the person actually does. Consider, for example, the situation where an individual has to take medicines to control high blood pressure. The measurement of that person's behavior would include behaviors that are related to the proper taking of the medications. What might that include? As a first step toward defining the behaviors we want to measure, we have to develop an operational definition of the behavior in question. We might include the actual sequence of events leading up to and including the taking of the medicines. So suppose that we had taught this patient that the best way to take blood pressure medicines regularly and properly was to include the medicine-taking as a regular part of ordinary behavior, such as eating supper. Our goal is to have the patient include taking his medicines as a part of a routine, so we could observe the individual and determine if he/she did take the medicines as part of supper. The point is that we are not only concerned with the "medicine-taking" behavior but within the larger complex of "supper-eating" behaviors. A good question to ask is, "Where do we draw the line between the behavior we want to measure and other, more global behaviors?" In other words, instead of stopping with "supper-eating," we could consider medicine-taking as part of the total daily activities. In this instance, the focus for behavior would be the much larger and more complex idea of "total daily activities." Focusing on "total daily activities" for measuring behavior would be like saying that the lowest common denominator for any number is 1; it is correct but not very helpful. In general, the more complex the behavior—complex in terms of context or components of the behavior—the more difficult it is to get measurement with reasonable validity and reliability. The shorter the time frame, however, the greater the risk of missing important parts of the context of the behavior in question. A compromise is needed. Behavioral measurement must include enough context to give meaning to observations, while at the same time the behavior to be observed must be rigorously defined.

Sampling Behaviors

Another key issue regarding measurement of behavior is sampling. Recall that earlier we were discussing an example where a parent was disciplining a child in the grocery store. If we were concerned with assessing parenting skills, we might decide to evaluate the parent based on the behaviors that we observed in the store. But would this really be reasonable? Do you believe that we could evaluate parenting skills based on a single public incident? This question brings up the larger issue: How much do we have to see of an individual's behavior to feel like we have enough data to reach a conclusion? If we are trying to evaluate a single behavior, what variety of context do we need to see to be able to understand the behavior? We might be able to justify basing our conclusion about parenting skills on behavior in the grocery store, because, as many parents have learned, taking small children to the grocery store can present a potent test of many parenting skills. We might assume that if the parent has skill to handle the "grocery store" behavior, they can handle virtually anything. On the other hand, how generalizable is grocery store behavior? Maybe the potential for embarrassment, assuming that embarrassment is an important motivator for behavior, changes the parent's behavior so that confrontations are avoided at all costs. We don't know how sensitive the parent is to embarrassment. Perhaps the parent's way of dealing with grocery store incidents is to wait to deal with incidents until he/she is finished and out of the store. Regardless, we have to decide how much faith we are going to put into the data that we can collect in the grocery store and decide if we need to collect data in other settings as well.

The **complexity** of the behavior and context is closely related to the sampling issue. Some behaviors are relatively simple. They are discrete in the sense that they are pretty much unconnected to other behaviors. Most behaviors are intimately connected to other things, however. Consider the example of compliance in taking medicine to control high blood pressure. Is this behavior simple or complex? A behavior is complex when it is one that is connected to many other parts of life. Simple behaviors are relatively unconnected to other things. Complex behaviors are much more challenging to assess than behaviors that are relatively unconnected.

Identifying Target Behaviors

Simple or complex, one of the first parts of assessment is to decide on a target behavior and derive a clear definition. In choosing a "target" behavior we are often in the position of having to choose one part of a complex behavior, with the assumption that the part we have selected for measurement represents the complex (complete) behavior. In other words, we try to find a part of a complex behavior that is "simple" to measure but gives us data to understand the behavior in its complexity. This is clearly a risky proposition, and one must choose wisely to select the "right" target behavior. Returning to our example of the person taking the blood pressure medicine, his/her adherence to the medical regimen includes several related behaviors. If we choose to keep track of one or two behaviors, which is probably all we could hope to do with any accuracy, then we do so with the assumption that the behaviors we measure are reasonably indicative of adherence. This is not done without risk, for we may have the bad judgment to select the wrong behaviors and miss the mark altogether. On the other hand, it is rarely feasible to measure all of the behaviors that we would wish: the art to behavioral assessment is in selecting parts of "behavioral chains" that accurately represent what we mean to measure.

TECHNIQUES FOR MEASURING BEHAVIOR

How do we go about actually measuring behavior? There are three primary methods that we can use: **direct observation, self-report,** and **indirect measurement.** Each of these methods has advantages and disadvantages, strengths and weaknesses.

Direct Observation

This method is probably the most obvious way to measure behavior but also often the most impractical. The most important features of this approach are that it limits measurement to behaviors that are objectively observable, but it eliminates the bias that often comes from using other methods of behavioral assessment.

Observability

To use direct observation, the behavior must be such that it can be identified and measured (counted usually) by a trained observer. This means that the context in which the behavior occurs must also be observable and that the observer must be able to pick out the target behavior. The observation must be systematic to produce an acceptable level of reliability. The time frame for observations must be designed so that a good sample of the behavior can be expected.

Definition of What is to be Observed

The definition for directly observed behaviors is not always easy to make clear. Suppose, for example, that you wanted to use direct observation to determine whether an individual had sharpened a pencil correctly. You could simply watch the process of "pencil sharpening," right? But what would you look for? What does "correct" pencil sharpening mean? A sharp point? Not grinding the pencil down unnecessarily? Neatness? You'd have to decide exactly what you want to observe and decide what you would label as evidence of "correct" or "incorrect" behavior. Remember that you want to observe the behavior, not participate. You can't measure the pencil or write with it to see how sharp the point is because that would be intervening in the process, and you simply want to observe people and record their behaviors systematically. The process of defining the behavior for observation is tricky. You can "overdefine" the behavior to the point that it can't be seen with any reliability (a pencil sharpened to the maximum without any unnecessary sharpening) or you can "under-define" (sharpening the pencil acceptably). The trick is to come up with a definition that gives the observer enough guidance to make sure that the right behavior is recorded with clarity and accuracy.

Validity of Observations

How long do you need to observe to make sure you get the best estimate of the behavior? Think about this a minute. You probably can't observe the individual in all settings and at all times when the behavior might occur, so you are collecting a "sample" of the behavior. How do you determine how to collect the sample? It would be best to carry out your observations throughout all of the available time and in all of the available places, but this is hardly ever feasible. Observers become fatigued and their accuracy falls off after long bouts of collecting data. They may also become bored and lose their concentration. A reasonable solution is to sample from the available times and locations. Conduct observations in "bursts" of five to ten minutes, three times per hour to prevent fatigue or boredom. Vary the place for observations if possible. Naturally, the expression of the rate or frequency of occurrence of the behavior should include consideration of the periods and places used for collection. It may be reasonable to average across all periods of observation in each site or, if the sites are all alike, to average across all periods as well as sites. If the frequency of occurrence of the behavior varied greatly among sites or time periods, then it is best not to average.

Reliability of Observations

Pretesting your procedures for conducting observations is very important. The usual procedure for pretesting includes use of at least two observers who carry out the protocol for the direct observation exactly as specified, but also completely independent of one another. It is crucial that neither observer know what the other records about what is seen. The results of the observations by the two observers are then compared.

The result of the comparison is labeled "inter-rater reliability" and can be expressed as the "percent agreement" between the observers. This statistic is calculated using the number of observation periods where the observers agreed divided by the total number of observation periods. (See Figure 7-1.)

Inter-rater reliability is calculated by comparing what two independent observers record as they watch the same individual performing the same behavior. The table shown below illustrates how the inter-rater reliability calculation would be carried out based on 25 observations made by two individuals.

		Observer #1		
		Behavior Observed	Behavior NOT Observed	Total
	Behavior Observed	12	2	14
Observer #2				
	Behavior NOT Observed	3	8	11
	Total	15	10	25

Total Agreement = 12 + 8 = 20
Agreement Reliability = Agreement/Total = 20/25 = .80

Figure 7-1. Inter-Rater Reliability

Inter-rater reliabilities of .85 or greater mean that there is relatively little disagreement among the raters. Lower inter-rater reliabilities are more suspect because they mean that there may be too much disagreement. Clearer definitions for the behaviors, in addition to more training and practice for the observers, is the only way to improve low reliability.

In sum, to carry out direct observation of behavior, the following specific steps are involved:

1. Define the behavior in question completely so that the observer can easily identify the target behavior within the context that it occurs;
2. Determine the time frame for observation based on needs for the sample;
3. Pretest the observational process to arrive at an acceptable level of reliability;
4. Carry out the behavioral observation, carefully recording the data in a systematic fashion.

Self-Report

Self-report is, as you might imagine, the method in which an individual reports on his/her own behavior. This is usually carried out in writing through keeping logs or journals of the target behaviors. Self-report can be a very effective means of collecting information on behaviors because it is easy and requires relatively little effort. As it turns out, though, self-report is not as easy to use as it sounds. The major concerns are indeed major; namely, the validity and reliability of the report. Is the patient being diligent in recording behaviors? Did the person use the correct definition to decide on "recordable" behaviors as you instructed? Did he/she "fudge" the recording due to embarrassment, or to please or show hostility to you? Did he/she forget to record the behaviors and then fill out the log all at once from memory?

Validity and Reliability of Self-Report

The validity issue in self-report is primarily concerned with the extent to which the individual understands and is able and willing to follow the instructions about recording the target behavior. Reliability is concerned with consistent compliance with recording. Validity is enhanced with a behavior that can be defined clearly, recorded simply, and not confused among other activities of daily living. Reliability is enhanced through designing a systematic method for recording behaviors, one that does not require interruption of the day's activities.

Reactivity

Designing a system for collecting behavioral data that is clear and easy to use still presents a change in the routine of most people. This change in routine, however subtle, usually causes some sort of reaction in the person. **Reactivity** is the phenomenon where the behaviors are changed primarily because of the attention given from self-report. Most people's behaviors will be altered to some degree by self-report and the alteration will be reflected in lower accuracy of their reports of behavior. To accommodate reactivity, a period of time for adjustment to the recording procedures should be planned. Given a few days or weeks, most people can be taught to record the target behavior accurately. As an example of this method, suppose you are trying to help a man lose weight. We know that people's weights are usually a product of how much they eat and how much exercise they get. We could use self-report as a means of collecting data from our patient on daily food intake and exercise. It would be wise to start with reporting on one behavior or the other, and add the second later. For our example, we'll design a self-report program for food intake. Remember, this is a log or journal that the man is going to complete on his own, so it has to be on the appropriate level. We would like to collect information on the number of calories consumed daily, but the individual is not going to be able to translate foods into calories as we would like. It makes more sense to have a record of the foods eaten and the amounts and leave the calorie calculations to us. The form shown in Figure 7-2 would be a good start. Adding the "activity" category would allow us to find out which foods were eaten as parts of meals and which were snacks. It would be best to have the person begin by keeping a record for a few days and then getting feedback from us. When we saw the individual next we could make any needed modifications to the self-report log (perhaps adding a space for describing the situation and other people present for snacks), reinforce the patient's compliance, and begin to get an idea of the man's pattern of eating.

Simple self-report forms like the one shown below can be used to collect information on behaviors that cannot be observed directly. One important limitation of the self-report approach, however, is the level of detail that can be collected. As the information on the form shows, we can learn what was eaten, but cannot learn how much from this self-report form. Making the form more detailed may improve the information collected, but the detail can also make the form too difficult for many people to complete.

Day and Time	Foods Eaten	Amount
Monday, 7:00am	Cold cereal, milk	1 bowl
Monday, 9:45am	Danish, coffee	1 danish
Monday, 12:30pm	Hot dog, diet soft drink	1 hot dog
Monday, 6:00pm	Spaghetti, salad, bread	1 serving
Monday, 9:00pm	Microwave popcorn, light beer	1 serving

Figure 7-2. A Self-Report Form for Recording Diet.

Indirect Measures

To avoid the pitfalls that are associated with use of direct observation and self-report, indirect measurement of behavior is sometimes necessary. Indirect measures are unmistakable signs that a specific behavior has occurred. An increase in body weight, for example, is an indicator that the individual has been eating too much for the amount of exercise that he/she gets. Some behaviors, such as overeating, smoking, and taking medicine as directed, for example, are behaviors that don't lend themselves to valid and reliable observation or self-reporting. For such situations, it makes better sense to rely on some type of indirect measure that reflects the behavior in question rather than rely on some other means of obtaining an estimate. Some individuals, in addition, are not capable or willing or able to participate in other methods for behavioral measurement because of poor eyesight, low literacy, etc.

Indirect measurement of behavior usually requires more resources and cooperation than self-report or direct observation. The data that are collected are usually more defensible in terms of reliability and validity, though. For example, suppose you wanted to assess smoking behavior in a patient. Direct observation of smoking would probably not reveal much more information than you could get from a thorough interview. Such observations might have some use in determining the role of other people or environmental influences on smoking frequency or intensity but might not be worth the time and effort needed to collect the data. Self-report would be useful but probably not entirely accurate. Smokers are renowned for their motivation to cover up their habit while "trying to quit," thus making the self-report information suspect. Collecting blood and measuring serum thiocyanate, a by-product from smoke inhalation, would be an unmistakable indicator of smoking. If you could manage to have the necessary resources and the cooperation of the patient (neither necessarily easy to get), then this method would provide good information about your patient's smoking behaviors.

We have presented three methods for measuring behavior in this chapter. Direct observation is useful for behaviors that we can see and, perhaps more importantly, that it makes sense to watch and count. Self-report is more versatile than direct observation in allowing us to make individuals aware of their own behaviors through self-observation. We are also able to collect data on behavioral patterns through self-report that are not possible with direct observation. Indirect observations measure the impact or outcome of behaviors.

READINGS

Haynes, S.N.: *Principles of Behavioral Assessment.* New York, Gardner, 1978.
Miller, L.K.: *Principles of Everyday Behavior Analysis.* Monterey, Brooks-Cole, 1975.

Williams, C.L., Eng, A., Botvin, G.J., Hill, P., and Wynder, E.L.: Validation of students' self-reported cigarette smoking status with plasma cotinine levels. *AJPH, 69*(12), 1272, 1979.

Part Two
PROGRAM EVALUATION:
THE APPLICATION OF MEASUREMENT

Chapter Eight

PROGRAM EVALUATION

In the first part of this book we presented the basic ideas underlying measurement. Now we've come to the point of applying the principles discussed in the first seven chapters to our central purpose: evaluation. To get started, this chapter will cover some of the essential ideas behind evaluation, as well as some of the classic motivations for carrying out evaluations. In addition, this chapter will present the dual philosophies that are in use in evaluation: traditional, quantitative evaluation and ethnographic, qualitative evaluation.

Chapter Nine will present and discuss the basic approaches to evaluation design and their strengths and weaknesses. Chapter Ten will continue by presenting the principles of data collection and analysis. Finally, the last chapter is devoted to ideas and techniques for presenting the results of evaluation effectively.

Definitions of Evaluation

The first question that we should deal with in this chapter is, What do we mean by evaluation? Evaluation is one of those terms that can have all sorts of meanings. The variety of uses of evaluation may make the basic meaning obscure, but when we use the word we mean that evaluation is a planned sequence of steps or parts that all contribute to arriving at a judgment about the status or value of health education or health promotion. The types of health education and health promotion programs that we want to evaluate, whether they be for screening, continuing education, prenatal education or something else, are all composed of parts that are supposed to work together to achieve some overall goal. The key elements in these programs are the steps, or parts, that are organized to add up to achieving the overall purpose.

Evaluation can be defined as the process of collecting information for the purpose of comparing something of interest, a program, to some standard of achievement that has meaning in a specific context. In this context, evaluation often consists of determining what a program achieved and comparing that with what was expected. Evaluation can be focused on the results of the program (summative evaluation) or on the development of the program itself (formative evaluation), or both.

Motivations for Evaluation

The approach used in carrying out evaluation depends on the needs of the situation. The methods used depend on the nature of the target of evaluation to a great extent, as well as what is wanted from the evaluation. Evaluation can have many different purposes. We can use evaluation as a means to assess accomplishments or diagnose shortcomings (of programs, individuals, or anything else for that matter), costs versus benefits accrued, political impact, short-term effects, long-term effects, and so on. We can even use evaluation to blunt controversial issues by collecting data that help make decisions. Likewise, evaluation is a common reason given to explain the collection of information that will be used to terminate employees and/or programs. In spite of the fact that evaluation is usually costly, disruptive, and sometimes very unpleasant, rational and objective use of evaluative information is accepted as the best path to making good decisions. The practice of flying by the seat of your pants and relying on gut instinct for making decisions has come into general disfavor. Ordinary people now commonly read reports of evaluations of product performance before they make a purchase. Business, education and many other fields have come to rely more and more on data from evaluations to provide guidance in making decisions. Decisions based on experience or intuition often seem less sound than those based on data. As a word of caution about blind reliance on data, however, even the most objectively collected information may be interpreted subjectively and presented in ways that allow for useful conclusions. The old adage "let the data speak for itself" may sound objective, but someone had to decide how to organize and present the data so that it could "speak" for itself. As a general rule, there is little spirit for following advice that contradicts experience, or even hunches. The basic models for evaluation that will be presented in upcoming chapters are modeled on designs used for experimentation in the "basic" sciences where objectivity is more or less assumed. Evaluation, based on objective scientific methods, is thought to rationalize or objectify the process of decision making, which in turn provides the decisions with defenses far more credible than "hunch" or "instinct." In essence, we evaluate to help make decisions.

The Role of the Evaluator

What is or should be the role of those who design and conduct program evaluations? The answer to this question depends to a great extent on the program to be evaluated, the setting in which it operates, and the professional relationship between the evaluator and the administrators and staff of the program. Probably the most basic considerations for program evaluators are the reasons for conducting the evaluation. If the reasons for the evaluation are not clearly understood by those wanting it, then those asked to do the evaluation will be unprepared to do their job. The first task of the evaluator, therefore, is to make sure that all parties are clear in their understanding of what the evaluation is to accomplish.

Less Precise Objectives	More Precise Objectives
Improve screening for cervical cancer in the target population	Increase the proportion of women, sexually active or age 18 or older, who have annual Pap smears
Ensure that women receive follow-up care in a timely manner	Increase the proportion of women with abnormal Pap smear results who return for follow-up care

Figure 8-1. Objectives with greater precision help evaluation of a cervical cancer prevention program.

A second, and equally important, area for concern is the nature of the goals and objectives of the program to be evaluated. Goals and objectives are the primary reference points for all measurement that is planned for program evaluations. In fact, the extent to which goals and objectives are well thought out and clearly articulated largely determines the pace of the evaluation. Programs with clear, appropriate and measurable objectives are much easier to evaluate than those without. Those without clear goals and objectives are far and away the majority, however. Figure 8-1 illustrates more and less precise objectives. Programs with clear and measurable objectives can be evaluated much more readily than programs with objects that are unclear. Figure 8-1 illustrates how precision could increase the usefulness of objectives for evaluation of a cervical cancer prevention program. The precision of objectives can be increased by specifying the target population, the timing of change, and unit of measurement. Specifying that the **proportion** of women at risk for cervical cancer is the focus of evaluation implies that merely counting Pap smears will not be adequate for this evaluation.

FOCUS OF EVALUATION

It is common to think of evaluation as always being primarily concerned with measuring the results of programs, such as how well program participants learned something or how much their behavior changed. Evaluation can be focused in a variety of directions. When evaluation focuses on the results from programs, it is often referred to as **outcome or summative evaluation.** The processes through which program results are produced are also of interest for evaluation, however. Evaluation that focuses on how programs operate is called **process evaluation.** In most cases, program evaluation includes both process and outcome evaluation components. Finally, evaluation can be focused on the specific tasks involved with developing programs. Such evaluation is termed **formative evaluation,** a name that indicates that we hope to use the results of evaluation to help form an effective program.

It might be surprising to learn that some programs are appropriately evaluated simply by counting how many patients were served, while other programs should be evaluated by carefully assessing how well they fit in with other related programs serving the same community. These differences point out that evaluation can be focused on different aspects of the program, the people it serves, or the overall system of health care. H.L. Blum (see "Readings" at the end of this chapter) shows the variety involved with evaluation by describing six aspects of programs that could be foci for evaluation. Blum labeled the six foci: **activity, meeting standards, efficiency, effectiveness, outcome validity and overall system appropriateness** (see Figure 8-2). As Figure 8-2 shows, the six foci of evaluation proposed by Blum fit together as a hierarchy of increasing complexity ranging from level 1, where the focus is limited to program activity, to level 6, overall system appropriateness, that focuses on the program as a component of a health care delivery system. Each level will be discussed in the sections that follow.

Activity

Focusing evaluation on program activities, level one evaluation, involves collecting and documenting information that demonstrates the operations of the program. Documentation can be a useful and important part of evaluation in providing examples of how the program operates. Such information can also be used as supplemental to other quantitative data collected for evaluation. Level one evaluation consists mainly of records of the program's activities. Correspondence, schedules, advertising to announce the program and recruit participants, newspaper articles and pictures of the program "in action" are all examples of level one evaluation data. Level one evaluation data can be used to determine whether the program is progressing in development as anticipated. Evidence of unanticipated problems with the program may surface with level one evaluation as well.

To illustrate level one evaluation, consider an example of a violence-reduction program developed for a school system. This program was requested by the school board in response to an outpouring of concern in the community. The superintendent of the school system responded to the school board by directing that a summer program be developed that would select and train one teacher to be a facilitator for a "safe schools" program. The central objective of the program would be to increase the resource base for dealing with violence in each school. Each teacher completing the training would serve as a resource person for the safe schools program in their school. Level one evaluation for this program could focus on documenting the activities of the program, in light of the overall plan. Activities that could be included in level one evaluation would be collecting program documents such as job descriptions for the teachers, announcements for recruitment of teachers, scheduling of the summer training program, and recording events within the summer program. Emphasis in level one evaluation would be placed on the activities that would signal that the program was not developing as anticipated. For example, if copies of program documents such as job descriptions could not be obtained, it could indicate that the program was not organized properly.

Standards

Level two evaluation focuses on the standards of performance expected from the program and asks whether such standards are being met. These standards range widely and can include such issues as the training of personnel to the acceptability of educational materials. Where level one evaluation documented program activities, level two evaluation compares the activities with the minimum standards expected of the program. Level two evaluation often focuses on administrative aspects of program development, implementation and evaluation. In many instances, for example, the funding of programs comes with requirements regarding such elements as the level of training required of personnel delivering program services and record keeping. Level two evaluation focuses attention on compliance with such requirements and helps to ensure that the program operates within established guidelines.

Continuing our example of the violence-reduction program introduced earlier in the discussion of "Activity," level two evaluation for this program could focus on ensuring that the summer training was provided by qualified instructors using the approved curriculum.

Efficiency

Evaluation focused on efficiency, level three, asks whether program outcomes are reasonable in light of the resources invested. Efficiency is commonly viewed in financial terms, but it can be viewed in other ways as well. For example, level three evaluation could address issues such as the number of students that should be in class if we want to develop maximum achievement by the learners. If it is agreed that individual instruction probably provides the best chance for getting maximum achievement but we cannot afford to provide individual instruction, then level three evaluation could address the compromises needed to arrive at the best achievement by the largest percentage of learners.

Level three evaluation of the violence-reduction program could address the issue of whether the summer training was able to reach the number of teachers anticipated in the time allotted. The results of this type of evaluation would provide information on the way that the training was organized. If the efficiency was low, perhaps the groups were too small or there were too few instructors available.

Effectiveness

Level four addresses effectiveness, perhaps the most commonly voiced objective of evaluation. Effectiveness is defined in terms of the objective of the program and asks to what extent the desired results are being produced in the target population by the program activities. Measurement related to level four evaluation focuses on the program objectives and may include such methods as collection of information from individuals, review of program records, or monitoring official statistics describing the target population. Chapter Nine will address many of the issues related to level four evaluation.

Level four evaluation of the school violence program would be based on assessing whether the resource base for dealing with violence in each school was increased. Answering this question would require that we have information on what other schools not receiving the program's services experience in dealing with school violence. Perhaps violence-related issues in schools in a neighboring district could be compared with those receiving the summer training, or rates of suspension or expulsion for violating school policy related to violence could be compared to assess the effectiveness of the program.

Outcome Validity

When evaluation is focused on outcome validity, the questions asked are directed at the effects of the program as a whole and its effects on the community. The question is not whether the program objectives were met but whether meeting the objectives resulted in the anticipated outcomes. Level five evaluation requires synthesis of information from sources other than the particular program under consideration. For example, if the school violence program was implemented as planned, outcome validity evaluation would focus on whether the additional resources helped the schools to address the problem of violence. If having the additional resources did not help the schools address violence, then the program would have little outcome validity. In other words, the program may have been developed correctly, but it was not an appropriate solution to the problem.

Overall System Appropriateness

Overall system appropriateness is the most global focus for evaluation and considers the influence of many different factors. Like outcome validity, level six evaluation involves observation of how related programs may interact. When programs function appropriately as a unit, community goals may be realized. Using the school violence example, the program would be evaluated positively in terms of overall system appropriateness if violence among the school population decreased. Such a decrease would not be due to the program alone, but the program would contribute positively to the system's solutions to the problem of violence.

From considering the six different foci for evaluation, it is apparent that the job of the evaluator changes as we move from level one to six because the number of factors increases and the questions become more abstract. The key point to remember is the focus of efforts should match with the desires of those asking for the evaluation. Be aware that those asking for evaluation may not have a specific focus for what they want. The lower level evaluations tend to be the least expensive in time and money. The higher level evaluations can be very complex and produce results that are difficult to clarify. Consultation with experts in particular fields may come in handy in figuring out how to focus the evaluation. With definitions, motivations, roles and levels of evaluation introduced, our attention now shifts to the basic philosophic underpinnings of evaluation of health education and health promotion.

QUALITATIVE AND QUANTITATIVE EVALUATION

One of the most important developments in the field of evaluation has been the influx of new qualitative methods. These methods, new to evaluation of health-related programs, arose from the social and behavioral sciences. Given that evaluation has historically been modeled on the methods used for investigation in the natural sciences (the scientific method, in other words), the introduction of qualitative methods has been a refreshing, quiet revolution. Qualitative methods aren't really new, but they are a new addition to the evaluation of health education and health promotion programs. It is very likely that evaluations of the future will be expected to include both qualitative and quantitative methods.

Two Distinct Paradigms

Quantitative evaluation is traditional. The goal for most evaluations is to collect measurable, preferably numeric, data attesting to the extent to which the goals and objectives of the program were reached. The emphasis is on measurement that is replicable and quantifiable. The **qual**itative approach is distinct from the quantitative. Instead of emphasizing the use of numerical measurement, the emphasis is on collection of information that addresses **how** and **why** the program met or failed to meet its goals and objectives. The information collected may be from a variety of sources using a variety of methods. Participant observations of process, open-ended interviews, case studies, focus groups, photography, life histories, and content analysis of documents are useful qualitative methods. How to actually employ these tools in program evaluation is discussed in more detail in Chapters Nine and Ten.

There is no question that good program evaluations almost always require that quantitative measurements be employed. It is our belief, however, that good evaluations also employ qualitative methods. This is because each method has certain strengths and weaknesses which to a certain extent are compensated for by the other method. As is indicated in Figure 8-3, the strengths of quantitative methods are that they produce hard, factual, reliable outcome data that are usually generalizable to some larger population. Where it is practical and feasible, evaluators should always attempt to collect such quantitative data in order to assess program effects. Figure 8-3 also suggests, however, that the strengths of qualitative methods are that they are process oriented, valid, assess clients' perspectives, holistic, and they assume a dynamic reality.

While there are exceptions, in general quantitative methods tend to focus on program results or outcomes, and qualitative methods tend to focus on program processes, i.e., program interventions. In short, quantitative methods tell the evaluator what a program's results were, and qualitative methods suggest why those results occurred. Health professionals, managers, and others should not only know which programs produce needed results but why such programs work or do not work. That is, in order to improve the practice of health education/promotion it is necessary to know the strengths and weaknesses of various interventions, not just whether they work or not. The assessment of such strengths and weaknesses is best done through the use of qualitative methods.

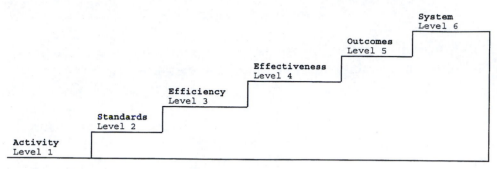

Figure 8-2. The levels of evaluation are like stair steps. Evaluation increases in complexity from level 1 to level 6.

Quantitative	Qualitative

• Deductive
  Verification and outcome oriented
	• Inductive
	  Discovery and process oriented

• Measurement tends to be objective	• Measurement tends to be subjective

• Reliable and Objective
  Technology as instrument (The evaluator is removed from the data.)
	• Valid and Subjective
	  Self as instrument (The evaluator is close to the data.)

• Generalizable
  The outsider's perspective
  Population oriented
	• Ungeneralizable
	  The insider's perspective
	  Case oriented

Figure 8-3. A Typology of Attributes of Quantitative and Qualitative Evaluation Methods

Program dynamics, the interaction of specific components of programs with clients, are readily assessed by using qualitative methods. These results are vital to program development, as they can be used to chart the course for development of successful health education interventions. They can indicate what the program was as it began, and how and why it evolved into the finished product. Quantitative measures are often most appropriate when a program has reached a "finished product" stage and has a certain level of maturity and stability. When the intervention has progressed through periods of growing pains, when objectives and methods have become tested and stabilized, then it is appropriate to quantitatively measure its effects.

Finally, quantitative methods fall short when the technology needed to measure specific knowledge, attitudes and behaviors does not exist. As we saw in earlier chapters, developing a questionnaire that is both valid and reliable is not an easy task. In fact, it is more difficult and more costly than most observers realize. In addition, there are many types of health attitudes and behaviors for which we simply do not have appropriate quantitative measures. For instance, in an evaluation of a program that provided instruction to children and adults about medical self-care, i.e., "how to be your own doctor, sometimes," no measures existed for the specific self-care skills that were taught. Two years (of the program's total four years) and several thousand dollars were required to develop, pretest and revise quantitative measures to adequately reflect what the program was teaching. The following example is included to illustrate the interplay between quantitative and qualitative approaches to development of evaluation.

AN EXAMPLE OF COMBINING QUANTITATIVE AND QUALITATIVE EVALUATION METHODS: THE COMPUTERIZED NUTRITION EDUCATION FOR WIC CLIENTS PROJECT

Allan B. Steckler and Robert M. Goodman

The Problem

The WIC (Women, Infant and Children's) program is federally funded and is administered by state and local health departments. The purpose of the program is to provide low-income women and their children with financial assistance for the purchase of milk and food. Federal guidelines require that WIC clients receive nutrition education as part of the WIC services. Over a period of years the Maternal and Child Health Section of the North Carolina state health department determined that many WIC clients who were served by local health departments were not receiving the required nutrition education. One reason that the nutrition education was not being delivered was because of the high case loads and relatively small number of qualified nutritionists who could provide the education.

The State Division of Maternal and Child Health wondered if the manpower shortage might be improved by using microcomputers to provide educational services to WIC mothers. The division applied for and received a federal grant to study this idea.

Project Goals

The primary emphasis of the evaluation study was to explore whether computers could improve health department capacities to provide required nutrition education sessions to clients enrolled in the WIC program. Other evaluation questions included the relative effectiveness of the computer vs. a nutritionist in providing the education; whether computers would be acceptable to clients; identification of organizational factors that would influence the successful use of the new technology; and relative cost. Also, the Division of Maternal and Child Health was concerned that nutritionists and health department clerks might not like the computers. If staff did not like clients using the computers, then the prospects of clients actually using them would be diminished.

Evaluation Design and Methods

Six county health departments in North Carolina participated in the study. Three health departments received computers and nutrition education software (the experimental group). In the remaining three health departments, nutrition education was taught by a nutritionist (the control group). These six health departments were selected by the State Division of Maternal and Child Health because they had been experiencing difficulty providing the required nutrition education visits for WIC clients. The study used both quantitative and qualitative methods. A summary of the methods used and results are presented in Figure 8-4.

Results

Qualitative data from the site visits, the interviews and the focus group discussions shed light on why clients liked the computer as a source of nutrition information: the computer information was comprehensive, the computer is non-judgmental, the client can work at her own pace, and the software programs were fun. The qualitative data also indicated that there was little resistance to computers by either the nutritionists or the health department clerks as had been feared by the state health department. Both nutritionists and clerks had a number of constructive ideas for how future software could be better tailored to WIC clients' needs. Overall, there were fewer barriers to introducing computers into the health departments than had been anticipated by the state health department, which meant that computers could be successfully used to provide nutrition education to WIC clients in local health departments throughout the state.

Quantitative Methods	Findings
Pre/post knowledge tests given to WIC mothers.	WIC mothers receiving either computer or nutritionist instruction had significant gains in knowledge.
Attitude questionnaires given to WIC mothers.	WIC clients were generally positive about both computer and nutritionist instruction.
Attitude questionnaires given to health department staff (nutritionists and clerks).	Staff supported the idea of computerized nutrition education for WIC clients.
Relative cost analysis (i.e., the costs of computerized education were compared to the costs of the nutritionist-led education).	Computers have the potential to deliver nutrition education less expensively than using nutritionists.
Qualitative Methods	**Findings**
Site visits to all six of the study health departments (i.e., both experimental and control sites).	Problems in placing computers and scheduling clients were observed.
Observations of the computer education and the nutritionist-led education.	Clients were able to use the computer, and they enjoyed the experience.
Open-ended interviews with WIC clients and with health department staff (health officers, nutritionists, nurses and clerks).	Staff suggested ways to improve the software and how to schedule clients to maximize use of computers; clients discussed what they learned or did not learn.
Focus Groups of WIC clients who had used the computerized nutrition education.	Clients made suggestions on improving use of computers, and what nutrition information they actually used.

Figure 8-4. Evaluation Methods and Sample Results, The WIC Computerized Nutrition Education Program

READINGS

Blum, H.L.: Planning for Health: *Development and Application of Social Change Theory.* New York, Human Sciences, 1974.

Borus, M.E., Buntz, C.G., and Tash, W.R.: *Evaluating the Impact of Health Programs: A Primer.* Cambridge, MA, MIT, 1982.

Green, L.W.: Evaluation and measurement: Some dilemmas for health education. *AJPH, 67*(2):155–161, 1977.

Reichardt, C.S., and Cook, T.D.: "Beyond Qualitative Versus Quantitative Methods." In Cook, T.D., and Reichardt, C.S., *Qualitative and Quantitative Methods in Evaluation Research.* Beverly Hills, Sage, 1979.

Chapter Nine

DESIGNING EVALUATION

This chapter presents the concepts and principles that underlie decisions about evaluation design. An evaluation design specifies the structure for collecting information needed to decide whether a program is functioning as it was intended. To illustrate what we mean by evaluation design, let's consider an example.

A community health education program was developed to prevent cervical cancer by providing education to women about the Pap smear and the importance of early detection. It was believed that education would contribute to increasing the percentage of women in the target community who received Pap smears on a regular basis. Reducing mortality from cervical cancer was the ultimate goal of the program, but those funding the program wanted evaluation to include a thorough assessment of the effectiveness of the program in changing behavior (increasing Pap smears), in addition to monitoring mortality. There were no predetermined standards for evaluating the effectiveness of the program. Rather, it was hoped that the program would increase the percentage of women in the target population having regular Pap smears, which would increase early detection of cancer, and thereby reduce mortality from cervical cancer. To carry out evaluation, it was decided to compare the percentage of women in the target population who had regular Pap smears before (time 1) and after (time 2) the health education program was implemented. To provide an estimate of what would have happened without any program, a similar target population was selected to serve as a control. The evaluation design is shown below in Figure 9-1.

		Time 1		Time 2
Community 1:	Receives Program	01	X	02
Community 2:	No Program	03		04

Figure 9-1. Evaluation design for the community cancer control program

As Figure 9-1 shows, the concept underlying the evaluation was that the difference between 02 and 01 would be greater than the difference between 04 and 03, indicating that a greater increase in the percentage of women reporting Pap smears occurred in the target population receiving the program. Likewise, the difference between 01 and 03 should be minimal, but the difference between 02 and 04 should be large if the program was effective. Data were collected by conducting surveys with randomly-selected samples of women from each target population.

Selecting a design for collecting information about the program is one of the most crucial of all of the decisions that are made in conducting an evaluation. Making good decisions about evaluation design requires awareness of the program and its objectives, the basic questions about the program that are supposed to be addressed by the evaluation, and many other issues that relate to the target population. The first part of this chapter will concentrate on presenting the basic concepts that underlie all evaluation designs, including essential definitions, an introduction to sampling, and factors that influence the validity of evaluation. This initial section is followed by sections that present traditional, quantitative evaluation designs and the qualitative approach. Following these discussions, a section on "Choosing the Best Design for your Evaluation" is included. Examples of quantitative and qualitative evaluations are included at the conclusion of the chapter.

Questions that Guide Evaluation Design

Evaluation can be designed to suit a variety of purposes. In the previous chapter, we introduced the notion of conducting evaluation on different levels. Recall that the levels of evaluation range from documentation of activity to inquiry about the appropriateness of the program in light of the system in place for delivering health services. The approach to evaluation changes from level to level, largely as a result of differences in the types of questions that are asked about programs. Figure 9-2 illustrates the types of questions that could be asked at various levels of evaluation.

Regardless of the level of evaluation wanted, key questions underlie evaluation:

1. Why is evaluation being done and what is it expected to show?
2. How will the results of evaluation be used?

Levels of Evaluation	$\rightarrow$	Questions
Level 6—Overall system appropriateness		Are changes produced by the program of benefit to the community?
Level 5—Appropriateness of outcomes		Are changes produced improving health of program participants?
Level 4—Program effectiveness		Is the program producing change as intended?
Level 3—Program efficiency		Is the program providing services at the predicted rate?
Level 2—Meeting minimum standards		Is the program serving the intended target population?
Level 1—Program activities occurring		Is there evidence that the program is functioning?

Figure 9-2. The levels of evaluation result in distinct Questions about programs and their effects on participants and the community.

3. What type of information about the program is needed for evaluation?
4. How should information about the program be collected to address the purposes of evaluation?
5. Once collected, how should information about the program be examined to address the purposes of evaluation?
6. Are there standards available that can be used in judging the information collected about the program?

Although each of the questions listed above suggests a different approach to evaluation, they share at least one common thread. The thread that links the questions is the basic proposition that evaluation is structured to collect information about what a program produced that can be compared with what was expected from the program.

Conceptual Bases for Evaluation

All experimental design, whether for evaluation or basic research, is rooted in a common conceptual foundation. This foundation is composed of ideas that form the logical basis for using data that have been collected from experiments to answer questions. These basic concepts involve **consistency, control,** and **sampling.**

Consistency

The first of the basic ideas that form the foundation for evaluation is consistency. Consistency in sample selection, data collection, and, perhaps most importantly, in providing the services of the program is essential to good evaluation. Without consistency in delivering a health education program, it is difficult to determine whether reactions are due to the program, the specific situation where the program was provided, or both. For health education programs, the subject of consistency raises a thorny issue. Health education programs are most effective, in theory at least, when they are tailored to individual needs. While such tailoring usually helps those receiving health education, it places limitations on evaluation because the effects of the program can only be understood if the changes in the program that were included in the tailoring are included in the evaluation. If tailoring is included, then the ability to draw conclusions about the program becomes limited because few individuals receive the same education. Program evaluations function best when the educational program is provided consistently.

Control

Perhaps the most basic question to be answered by evaluation is whether the program was effective. Another way of stating this question is to ask whether the program made things turn out any different than they would have if the program had not been in existence. We must have a standard for comparison to be able to answer this fundamental question. This issue may seem almost intuitive and very obvious, but it has profound implications for evaluation design. If we want to know whether the program made a difference, we have to know what we mean by difference. The simplest way to come up with a definition for difference is to record what occurs in a group **not** exposed to the program. The group not exposed is said to **control** for the effect of the program in the population. It is important to note that although we have limited our discussion to two groups, we could have multiple groups receiving the program and acting as controls. Regardless of the number of groups involved, we must assume that the two groups are alike except for the influence of the program.

The notion of control is easily generalized beyond the control group application to include controlling for any factors related to composition of the groups that could influence the outcome of the evaluation. It is common, for example, to include consideration of the effects of factors such as the age distribution of the groups included in the evaluation or other factors that might influence the outcomes from a program (see Figure 9-3). If we were evaluating a cancer prevention program, for example, we might want to control for the age of the women in the program. Figure 9-3 shows how the information about the number of women attending a screening clinic before and after implementation of the program might be recorded, controlling for age and whether the women lived in an urban or rural area.

In summary, the concept of control addresses the need to have information to use for judging whether and how those who participated in the program are different from others who did not participate. Control groups are included in evaluation designs to provide a standard for comparison. We can also design evaluation with the intention of controlling for the effects of factors that influence the effectiveness of the program.

Sampling

In an ideal world, evaluation data would be collected from all of the potential participants in a program. Such an ideal is impractical, since there is no way for all potential users of most programs to be identified. Even if we could identify them, we probably couldn't collect evaluation data from them as we would want. If we cannot collect data from all the potential program participants, and we have to do evaluation nevertheless, then we have to find another way to collect information that can be used for evaluation. In this situation, our goal becomes to collect data that will allow us to estimate what the responses would have been if we had contacted each person in the population of potential program participants. The most practical way to reach this goal is to select a sample of people to represent the population of potential program participants and collect our information from them. The principal limitation of this approach is that we will have to assume that the responses that we collect from the sample accurately represent what we would have gotten if we had information from everyone in the population. In view of this assumption, we have to be careful about selecting the sample, because collecting information from part of the population introduces **bias** into the evaluation. Bias is any factor or occurrence that introduces systematic error. By limiting collection of information about a program to a sample instead of including all potential participants, we run a risk of unknowingly including factors in the evaluation that influence our conclusions but really should

	Percent having Pap smears Before Implementation	Percent having Pap smears After Implementation
Age < 40		
Urban		
Rural		
Age 40-49		
Urban		
Rural		
Age 50-59		
Urban		
Rural		
All Ages		
Urban		
Rural		

Figure 9-3. The illustration below shows how recording of reports from program participants about Pap smears can be recorded with categories that control for age groups and urban/rural place of residence.

have no role in the evaluation. These factors become added into the evaluation because of the characteristics of those providing information, the way the information is collected, or both. For example, suppose we were to evaluate whether a public health education program focusing on smoking reached a low-income target audience. Collecting information for the evaluation from those telephoning the project office to get more information about how to stop smoking might seem like a convenient and efficient way to collect information for the evaluation. If we found out whether the callers had seen, heard about, or read any of the program's educational materials, then we might conclude that the program contributed to decisions to make the telephone calls. While such a strategy would be likely to provide some useful information about how the program worked, the information would only be from those with access to a telephone and motivation to call. People in the target population without access to a telephone would not be included among those providing information, and therefore, any estimate of the impact of the program based on the telephone calls would be biased. Eliminating bias in this situation would require finding ways to ensure that all persons who came into contact with the program materials had an equal chance to provide information for the evaluation. To repeat, any factor that alters the chance for any participant to provide information injects bias into the evaluation of a program.

In practical terms, it is probably impossible to foresee every source of bias, so a reasonable approach is to select a sample of people from the population where every potential participant has an equal chance of providing information for evaluation. When each individual in the population has an equal chance of being selected, the sample is said to be an **equal probability sample.** Unbiased estimators are not necessarily **representative** of the population, however. Just because every individual has an equal chance of being selected, it is not certain that all subgroups in the population will be included in the sample. By chance, the sample could overrepresent or underrepresent important subgroups in a population which could be troublesome for the evaluation. Solutions to the problem of representativeness of the sample will be addressed later in this chapter.

Applying the Principles of Sampling

We use sampling to simplify evaluation, to save time and expense, and because we have learned that getting the type of information that we need does not require that we interact with each and every member of a population. In essence, sampling theory provides the basis for developing estimates of the precision of the information that we collect when we only include some of the population in the evaluation.

Sampling rules must provide the foundation for the process used in making selections from the population. Such rules guide many of the decisions about sampling, and bridge the needs of the evaluation and the characteristics of the target population. For example, if the evaluation needed to reflect the age distribution of the target population, the sampling rules might stipulate that the numbers of individuals selected in age groups 18–44, 45–64 and 65 and over should reflect the percentage of people in the target population in those age groups. On the other hand, the evaluation could stipulate that specific areas of the target population (housing developments, for example) be specifically included in the sample. Specifications on age and place of residence are usually motivated by a need to ensure that a sample is representative of a population.

A **probability sample,** commonly mislabeled as a "random sample," is one where each member of the population has a known chance of being selected. Evaluation has a strong foundation when it is based on unbiased samples, but it is important to recognize that the sample selected might or might not adequately represent specific parts of the population. By providing rules to guide the selection process, we can ensure that key parts of a population are included in the probability sample. The principle of unbiased selection remains important whether or not restrictions are placed on the selection process. To minimize bias, samples should be selected where each member of a population, or a part of a population, has an equal chance of being selected.

The process of selecting a sample begins with a **sampling frame.** The sampling frame describes the population to be sampled and, in theory at least, identifies each member. If we were making selections by telephone, then our sampling frame would include the numbers of every telephone in the population. Conceivably, we could dial each number and reach every member in the sampling frame by telephone. Considering an example of an evaluation focusing on school classrooms, we could begin with a sampling frame that included all schools in the district (see Figure 9-4). In general, the more detail that is included in the sampling frame, the greater its utility. Detail can help to decide which elements should be excluded, what types of groupings should be developed, and how the sample can be drawn most efficiently. Sampling frames of telephone numbers that are designed to focus on households, for example, may be organized by digits so that those reserved for institutions, businesses, or government can be eliminated, saving many telephone calls.

Once a sampling frame has been established, the selection strategy can be decided. There are several strategies, or methods, that are used in sampling. The basic sampling strategies include selection at random or systematically from the population as a whole, or selection using strata

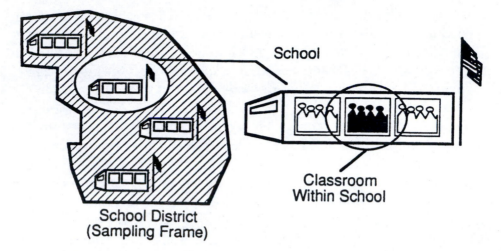

School

Classroom
Within School

School District
(Sampling Frame)

Figure 9-4. To collect information from a classroom, the sampling process would begin with establishing a sampling frame. Schools could be selected at random, from predetermined strata, or systematically. Classrooms could also be selected from within schools at random, from strata or systematically.

or clusters within the population. The choice among these approaches depends on what is to be estimated and the characteristics of the population. (Detailed discussion of sampling theory is beyond the scope of this text. A list of likely sources for further reading is included at the end of this chapter.)

Random and Systematic Selection

When we select subjects or objects for data collection "at random," we mean that there is no rule or specific reason, except chance, that decides whether an individual is selected. Each of the potential subjects has the same chance of being selected for study, and nothing was done to sort the subjects before selection. Selection at random from the entire population of potential program participants, commonly known as "simple random sampling," requires that each member of the population have the same chance of being selected. The process of random sampling begins with developing a sampling frame that includes all members of the popula-tion and identifies each member with a unique numerical identifier. A list of numbers is then selected from the sampling frame at random. The random selection of numbers can be carried out using a table of random numbers, calculator or computer program that produce lists of random digits. (Detailed descriptions of procedures for selecting random samples are included among the sources listed at the end of this chapter.) The final step in the process is accomplished by matching the numbers identifying each member of the population with the numbers selected in the sample. Figure 9-5 illustrates a sampling frame with a population of 90 individuals, from which 12 were selected for interviewing.

001	011	021	031	041	051	061	**071**	081
002	012	022	032	042	**052**	062	072	**082**
003	013	**023**	033	043	053	063	**073**	083
004	014	024	034	044	054	**064**	**074**	084
005	015	025	**035**	**045**	055	065	075	085
006	016	026	036	046	056	066	076	**086**
007	017	**027**	037	047	057	067	077	087
008	018	028	**038**	048	058	068	078	088
009	019	029	039	049	059	069	079	089
010	020	030	040	050	060	070	080	090

*Numbers in boldface type were those selected

Figure 9-5. Each member of a population of 90 individuals was listed on the sampling frame. A sample of 12 of the members was selected at random to be interviewed.

When the population of potential program participants is very large, developing a sampling frame that identifies each member, assigns them a number, and selects them is impractical (or impossible). For example, suppose that we wanted to select a sample of homeowners in a large community at random and find out what they had learned about radon testing after a series of television broadcasts and newspaper articles on the subject. If we could collect the needed information by telephone interview, then we could select a random sample of homeowners with telephones. The sample would be selected from all possible combinations of digits that could be telephone numbers. We could reduce the number of calls made if we could identify combinations of digits that would not connect us with the population that we wished to sample, such as government telephone numbers, institutions and businesses. Computers can easily generate such lists of digits. The numbers would be called and interviews carried out with homeowners. Bias could be introduced into the sample selected from the fact that those who were interviewed were not representative of the entire population but instead were selected from those who had a working telephone and were available to answer the telephone when the interviewer called. To reduce bias from people with telephones but not at home, we could make calls at varying times of the day and evening and require at least three attempts at different times of the day before a number was skipped. The bias from those in the population not having working telephones and from residences with more than one telephone number, residences where the telephone was temporarily out of service, or situations where the homeowner refused to participate would remain as unsystematic error. The cost and convenience of the telephone method must be weighed against the unsystematic error to determine whether telephone interviews are worthwhile. The same approach would be used if the data were collected by mail or personal interview.

Systematic sampling is a variant on selection at random. Systematic sampling is preferred in many cases because it is easier to implement than random sampling. Simply stated, in systematic sampling every kth person is included in the sample (see Figure 9-6). Suppose that we are concerned with evaluating the services of a family planning clinic. The patients of the clinic, mostly women, come in from the community and surrounding areas and are served on a first-come, first-served basis, and there is no practical way to use random selection. An alternative approach would be to select patients to include in the evaluation as they come to the clinic for services. It would not be necessary to interview every patient because it is highly likely that many of them would provide essentially identical information. To structure selection of which patients to interview, we need to have an estimate of the number of patients that will be seen during the evaluation period and the number of interviews that are wanted. Suppose that the clinic sees an average of 475 patients per month and that the administration decides that 50 interviews will be needed. If we selected every 9th patient and carried out an interview, we would have at least 50 interviews completed in one month. By adopting a plan of selecting every 9th patient to interview, we are planning a systematic sample, where k = 9. If we divide the estimated number of patients per month, 475, by k, we can expect to complete at least 52 interviews. To begin selection, we need to select the first patient at random. We could do this by establishing a start date for the evaluation, consulting a table of random numbers and selecting a number to identify the first patient to be interviewed. This patient could be identified by numbering patients as they registered for services and matching the number selected with those assigned to the patients.

Systematic sample size = N/k,
where N = total number eligible for selection, and
k = sampling interval. For N = 475 and k = 9,
the expected sample size would be 475/9 = 52.78

001	011	021	031	041	051	061	071	081
002	**012**	022	032	**042**	052	062	**072**	082
003	013	023	033	043	053	063	073	083
004	014	**024**	034	044	**054**	064	074	**084**
005	015	025	035	045	055	065	075	085
006	016	026	**036**	046	056	**066**	076	086
007	017	027	037	047	057	067	077	087
008	**018**	028	038	**048**	058	068	**078**	088
009	019	029	039	049	059	069	079	089
010	020	**030**	040	050	**060**	070	080	090

*Numbers in boldface type were those selected

Figure 9-6. Each member of a population of 90 individuals was listed on the sampling frame. The number 6 was selected at random, signifying that every 6th individual would be selected.

Random and systematic sample selection can be carried out from the entire population. In addition, we can consider subunits of the population and carry out random or systematic sampling within each subunit. It may be necessary to use subunits to ensure that the sample represents the population adequately. In addition, using subunits may make sample selection and data collection less expensive and time consuming than considering the population as a whole. The following sections on stratified and cluster sampling illustrate two ways of using subunits in sampling.

Stratified Sampling

Stratified sampling is used when it is important for the sample to be representative of the population and it is unlikely that selection from the population as a whole will work well. The procedures involved with stratified sampling include establishing a sampling frame that includes clear identification of the categories (strata) that are to be included, followed by sampling within the strata (see Figure 9-7). The sampling within the strata may be carried out at random or systematically. If we wished to carry out sampling stratified by age, for example, we would develop a sampling frame that specified the population in terms of age groups and then carry out sampling by age. This procedure would ensure that the sample represented the age categories as needed.

Cluster Sampling

In some situations it is not possible to list every member of the population, but it is possible to identify groups that are parts of the population. If we can select a sample of groups, we can develop sampling frames of the groups and select our samples from within each group. In this way, we can devote time to developing a listing of each group member and, using a random or systematic strategy, select an unbiased sample of the population. To illustrate how cluster sampling might work, consider an example of evaluating a school health education program on AIDS prevention. To evaluate whether the program influenced knowledge and attitudes toward safe sex practices, it would be necessary to have students complete a questionnaire. Developing a sampling frame for all of the students who received the program would be too costly and time consuming, so we could consider students in particular classes as clusters and select a sample of clusters to include in the evaluation. (Refer to Figure 9-4 for an illustration of cluster sampling applied to a school situation.) The selection of clusters could be carried out by developing a list of all clusters, or a list of all of the 9th grade health education classes that are held in all schools in the school district. From the list, a sample of classes could be selected at random or

Age Groups

| | 18-44 | | | | 45-64 | | | 65+ |

001	011	021	031	041	051	061	071	081
002	**012**	022	032	042	052	062	072	**082**
003	013	023	033	043	053	063	**073**	083
004	**014**	024	**034**	044	**054**	064	074	084
005	015	025	035	045	055	065	075	085
006	016	026	036	046	056	066	076	086
007	017	027	037	047	057	**067**	077	087
008	**018**	028	**038**	048	058	068	078	**088**
009	019	029	039	049	**059**	069	079	089
010	020	030	040	050	060	070	080	090

*Numbers in boldface type were selected

Figure 9-7. The sampling frame shown before includes 90 individuals grouped into three age groups. Samples of 4 individuals were selected* at random within each strata to ensure that the overall sample would be balanced by age. Systematic sampling could have been used.

systematically. Each class would be defined as a cluster. Once the sample of clusters was identified, the students in each class would comprise a sampling frame, and random or systematic sampling could be used to select individual students. Depending on the school district policies, it would be likely that the parents of the individual students would need to give their permission for their children to participate in the evaluation. In this case, cluster sampling would be an economical approach because of the cost in time and money of developing a sampling frame for the entire population and interacting with each student. The savings in time and money from developing sampling frames within classes makes the cluster sampling approach attractive.

Validity of Evaluation

Recall that in Chapter Three, "Accuracy of Measurement," we discussed the concepts of validity and reliability at length. That discussion was oriented toward measurement. The concepts of validity and reliability are also crucial to evaluation. We noted earlier that good measurement depended to a large extent on good reliability and validity; for evaluation to be credible, it must also be reliable and valid.

Recall that earlier we stated that validity was the extent to which an instrument measured as intended. In a similar vein, a valid evaluation is one that measures the program's accomplishments as intended. The phrase "as intended" here not only includes the intentions of the evaluators but also incorporates the concepts of evaluation: it could be rephrased as "in accordance with the principles of good experimental design." We can subdivide validity according to the applications of the evaluation and consider **internal** and **external** validity.

Internal and External Validity

Internal validity is the extent to which an evaluation measures the accomplishments of a program as specified by its own goals or objectives. In other words, an internally valid evaluation is one that demonstrates the extent to which a program produced the effects in the target population as predicted. External validity is concerned with generalizability. Where internal validity is focused on the accomplishments of a program in terms of expectations of producing change in a specific target population, external validity is concerned with the likelihood of achieving similar results in other populations.

A useful way to view internal and external validity is in terms of the factors and forces that may become limitations on the conclusions that may be drawn from evaluation. From the point of view of the evaluator, limitations on internal and external validity are factors that should be included as "hedges" in conclusions about the program's effects and uses. Recalling that internal validity is the extent to which the program produced the changes as planned, what factors or forces are most likely to limit conclusions about program effects? Keep in mind that the factors and forces listed below become threats to validity because we cannot estimate the extent to which they influence the outcomes.

Limitations on Internal Validity

History and/or Maturation. Suppose an event outside of the control of the program produces change in the target population just like that expected from the program's activities? Could you tell which source produced the change? Probably not. An historical event produced change that provided a competing explanation for the change you observed in the target population. Likewise, the target population's experience with the subject matter often increases with exposure to the program (not to mention through the passage of time alone), and the simple exposure may also produce change. As an illustration, do you suppose that American women were affected by the extensive coverage of Mrs. Betty Ford's experience with breast cancer while her husband was President? If your program was designed to urge women to begin practicing Breast Self-Exam, how much of the response from your target population might be attributed to knowledge of Mrs. Ford's experience?

Testing and/or Instrumentation. Is it possible that the results that you get from evaluation are due to the subjects' reactions to the methods used for measurement, or the mere fact of measurement, rather than the intervention? Psychologists refer to this phenomenon as "reactivity"—when behaviors or attitudes change as a reaction to measurement. As an example, do you think that people's feelings and behaviors about child abuse might be affected by filling out a questionnaire about their own child-rearing practices? Might they be motivated to examine their behaviors or change the descriptions of their behaviors? There are two distinct sources of such effects: testing and instrumentation. A **testing** influence is one that comes from the mere fact of measurement of a particular type in a particular target population. The influence of **instrumentation** is that from a specific method of measurement. For example, asking Spanish-speaking people to complete a questionnaire written in English is likely to produce invalid results.

Selection. Results from evaluation are often dependent on data that can be collected from clients of the program. Using willing clients as sources of data is sometimes carried out with the assumption that these clients are representative of the clientele that is usually served by the program. In fact, they may be a highly select group that is willing to provide information, very distinct from the rest of the clients of the program. When those used for evaluation are not representative of the clientele, then conclusions from the evaluation may not be valid.

Differential Attrition. Many types of evaluation utilize designs where subjects are divided into groups. The groups make comparison possible. The value of the comparison hinges on the comparability of the groups. Any forces that act to make the groups less alike work against the purposes of the evaluation. Differential attrition occurs when individuals are lost from groups in ways that make the groups unequal. In the usual case we don't know why people dropped out; they may be those that the program served the best or those with whom the program failed.

Regression Artifacts. This cumbersome term describes a rather simple idea. Suppose that in order to carry out an evaluation, you needed to recruit subjects from the clientele of the program. As a basis for recruitment, you decide to use scores on a test that was administered to all clients. Based on chance occurrence, it is probable that many of the scores don't really reflect the true status of the subject but are for some reason extreme. Maybe the subject was tired or angry or happy on the day he/she was tested and the score reflected this altered state. On retesting, such subjects' scores would be much closer to the average score of all similar subjects. So you select your subjects for the evaluation based on scores that include uncontrolled factors. If the scores used for selection are indeed extreme and the values truly reflect the state of the subject, then the evaluation will be unaffected. On the other hand, if the extreme scores are invalid, then the evaluation will be greatly influenced and perhaps invalid!

Limitations on External Validity

As you recall, external validity is the extent to which the results of the evaluation can be generalized to other populations. Once again, this type of validity can be better understood if you consider the factors and forces that pose threats. Logically, anything that threatens internal validity also poses a threat to generalizability. Overall, any force that changes the way the program operates to the point that the results of an evaluation would produce different results in a different setting will threaten external validity. The major threats to external validity include the following:

Randomness/Representativeness. Since external validity is concerned with the generalizability of results, it only makes sense to consider the population used for the evaluation as a primary concern for this type of validity. To the extent that the population used for evaluation is representative of the population for which the program is intended, the results of the evaluation are externally valid. From a scientific point of view, this may be demonstrated by a "random" sampling process used to select the population used for the evaluation. From an applied point of view, however, representativeness may be more important than strict randomization. The bottom line is that the results of the evaluation are only applicable to other groups like the one used for the evaluation.

Selection-Treatment Interaction. External validity may also be limited by the extent to which the program specifically affected those selected for evaluation. If the program has effects specific to those included in the evaluation, the results will only be narrowly applicable.

Testing-Treatment Interaction. In some cases the way in which evaluation data are collected (testing) may influence or be influenced by the program. Any condition within the program or the testing that would not be duplicated in another setting limits external validity.

The art and science of evaluation becomes evident in the selection and implementation of the "correct" design for a given situation. The limitations on internal and external validity provide guidance that may be of help in selecting the best design. At the basis of selection, however, are the goals of the program being evaluated and the goals of the evaluation itself.

Quantitative Evaluation Designs

As mentioned earlier, the basic types of evaluation designs will be discussed here. There are many more, of course, but most are variants on the basic types that we will present here. (For a more extensive presentation of research designs, consult the readings at the end of this chapter.) With regard to any type of evaluation design, there are two basic principles that you should always keep in mind. First, all designs are intended to enable you to get an estimate of some effect (a "dependent" variable) that you think will be produced by the program (an "independent" variable). Second, the reliability and validity of the estimate that you get depends not only on the design that you use but on the methods of measurement. That is to say, you get what you pay for, so to speak. The more rigorous the design and more precise the measurement, the more valid and reliable the estimates. The quantitative evaluation designs presented here may be implemented as "true experiments" or "quasi-experiments." True experiments are denoted by random assignment of participants to the group. Quasi-experiments use the same designs but do not use random assignment. Most evaluations of health education and health promotion programs use quasi-experimental, because randomization is often impossible in the settings where these programs operate.

An interesting idea that you should keep in mind while reading about the designs is that all of the "analytic" designs, those that are concerned with numerical measurement, have their roots in agricultural experimentation (no pun intended). Early experimenters developed principles that are now basic to experimental design through their experience with seed varieties, water, and fertilizers. The importance of this note is that the control that is possible in agricultural experimentation is usually not feasible in evaluation of programs that involve humans. Consequently, some of the principles that you will read, in other books as well as here, are only rarely used in evaluations that involve people.

Before-and-After Designs

The most intuitive approach to designing evaluation is based on the deceptively simple question, "What changed during the time that the program was functioning?" This approach is used widely and turns out to be the approach to evaluation that is often expected by administrators as well as practitioners. Simple questions rarely have simple answers in program evaluation, however. In addition to the question about changes that occurred during the program, we could ask some additional questions such as: "Would change have occurred even if there had not been a program?"; "How does the change that was detected compare with what we expected?"; "If we were to repeat the program, how sure are we that we could get the same result, less or even greater change?"; "Would we expect similar results in a different population?" and so on. As you can see, our simple question about before-and-after differences could very easily turn out to be quite complicated. One way to sort out some of the complications comes from comparing change occurring in those receiving the program with those not receiving the program. The experience of those not receiving the program becomes a standard to judge the results obtained from those who received the program. Let's see how these might work in diagram form.

Figure 9-8 illustrates a before-and-after (also known as "prepost") evaluation design. As shown in Figure 9-8, we have a measurement at time 1 (01), an intervention X, and a repeat measurement at time 2 (02). We expect measurement carried out at 02 and 01 to be different because of the influence of the program. Importantly, we must assume that 01 and 02 are independent. That is, there was no connection between the

	Time 1 (Before)	Program Implementation	Time 2 (After)
Group 1	01	X	02

Figure 9-8. Before-and-after evaluation design

two measurements. If there is a connection, for example, if at 02, some remembered what they said or wrote at 01, then the comparison between 01 and 02 will be confusing to interpret. We won't be able to tell how much difference or similarity between 01 and 02 to attribute to the program and how much to attribute to memory. In general, the basic limitations of the before-and-after design with no comparison is that we can't be sure if any difference we find between 01 and 02 was due to the program, other forces at work, or if the change would have occurred regardless of the program. It is possible that the difference observed between 01 and 02 would have occurred without the program. In fact, it is possible that the difference between 01 and 02 would have been greater without the program!

To improve the before-and-after design shown in Figure 9-9, data from a similar group not receiving the program could be collected to allow us to learn about changes occurring among those not receiving the program.

	Time 1 (Before)	Program Implementation	Time 2 (After)
Group 1	01	X	02
Group 2*	03		04

*(Control Group)

Figure 9-9. Before-and-after evaluation design with a control (comparison) group

Figure 9-9 shows how we can add a "control group" to the basic before-and-after design. As Figure 9-9 shows, we have added Group 2, with measurements 03 and 04 that are carried out just as for Group 1. The control group enables us to estimate what would happen if there was no program given. With the evaluation design shown in Figure 9-8, we expected a large difference between 01 and 02 and did not consider a control group at all. For quasi-experimental designs, the more similar the two groups at the outset, the better our estimate of the effects of program X. We could improve the design and reduce concern about similarity between the groups if we would allocate subjects to the two groups at random from one pool of subjects.

Analysis of data collected from before-and-after designs with a control group involves investigating the differences between the groups, (02 versus 04) versus (01 versus 03). In other words, we need to focus on three contrasts in the analysis. First, is there evidence that the groups were different before the program was implemented? Second, is there evidence that the groups were different after the program? Third, is the difference of before versus after different between the groups? Let's illustrate how this works using an example. The evaluation of a community-wide cervical cancer prevention program included interviews with random samples of women from two communities. One community received the program and the other served as a control. One of the items in the evaluation asked whether the women had seen mass media information on cervical cancer prevention. The data are summarized in Figure 9-10, using the number of women who reported having seen information on cervical cancer.

	Before Implementation (%)	After Implementation (%)
Program Community	54	75
Control Community	56	60

Figure 9-10. Percent of women in the program and control communities reporting that they were aware of cervical cancer prevention information in the community before and after the program was implemented.

Analysis of the information shown in Figure 9-10 would contrast .54 vs .56, .75 vs .60, and (.75 vs .54) vs (.60 vs .56). The statistical analysis of these data is treated in many statistics texts under topics such as "differences in proportions" and will not be repeated here. The goal of statistical analysis, however, is to determine the probability of observing the same differences again in a similar situation by chance alone. If the differences are large enough, then we conclude that they were not the result of chance but occurred because of purposeful action—perhaps the program. In sum, large differences between program and control group(s) support the idea that the program had succeeded in making women aware of cervical cancer prevention.

An important consideration effecting before-and-after evaluation designs is the risk of the before measurement contaminating the after measurement. If the time between measurements is short, the chance that the after measurement will be influenced by the before measurement is great. As you may recall, such influence poses a serious threat to the evaluation because it means that the before-and-after measures may not be independent. People may remember their answers from their initial experience with the evaluation and may decide to give the same answers, or they may decide that they should not give the same answers twice even if they have not changed. Regardless, unsystematic error is introduced to the evaluation when the time between before-and-after measurements is too brief. A minimum of two weeks is usually recommended to reduce the chance of contamination. Figure 9-11 shows an approach that has been used to deal with the problem of independence between before-and-after measures. The design shown in Figure 9-11 is known as an "after-only" or "posttest-only" design because it eliminates the before measures.

	Time 1 (Before)	Program Implementation	Time 2 (After)
Group 1		X	01
Group 2*			02
*(Control Group)			

Figure 9-11. Posttest-only evaluation design

The posttest-only design relies on the notion that groups 1 and 2 started out the same and that any differences between 01 and 02 were produced by the program, X. Analysis of data from the after-only design involves a comparison of the results of measurement among those who received the program with those who did not.

The limitations of the after-only design are pretty apparent. There was no assessment of the status of participants and controls before the program was introduced. If it can be assumed that those receiving the program and the controls are representatives of the same target population, then there would be no reason to suspect that those receiving the program were different from the controls before the program was introduced. If such an assumption cannot be made with confidence, however, then the after-only design is risky. The after-only type of design is strongest when there is unbiased assignment to the groups. If assignment to the groups is carried out at random or systematically, then in theory, potential biases will be distributed among both groups.

The before-and-after designs and after-only designs shown here are illustrative of a host of similar approaches. Regardless of the design, though, the approach remains the same: assessment of the change that occurred during the time that the program was functioning. Addition of a control strengthens the assessment of the effects of the program because it enables the evaluator to also estimate what would have happened in a similar group if a program had not been present.

Evaluation of Trends

The concept of "before versus after" as an approach to evaluation can be extended to consider multiple points in time. When we consider multiple points in time, we have the ability to monitor trends. Such an approach to evaluation, often referred to as "trend analysis," requires more time for data collection but carries the advantage of measuring change within a context that may be changing itself. This approach is particularly useful when the timing of program effects cannot be predicted precisely, when the effect may fall off rapidly, or when the effect occurs in cycles.

To use the trend analysis approach to program evaluation, we must be able to carry out measurement repeatedly and measurements need to be carried out before the program is implemented. Because of the need for repeated measurements, it is common to use information that is routinely collected as data for trend analyses. Using data that are routinely collected also reduces the problem of contamination of measurements that arises when measurement is repeated.

Case Studies

Case studies are a third category of approaches to program evaluation. In the approaches outlined previously, we emphasized planned measurement as the means for distinguishing between before and after as well as for changes in trends. The "case" approach emphasizes collection of data that describes and measures change. The case study approach is often selected when there is only one group to be studied as in a demonstration of a new program. The data are often anecdotal records and those from systematic observations, as well as measures of knowledge, attitudes and behaviors. The goal of the case study method is to describe and explain the experience of a subject or a group of subjects as they experience a health education program without the use of experimental methods (dividing participants into groups, pre- and post-measurement). While case study evaluations often incorporate traditional measurement of the subjects' knowledge, attitudes and behaviors, the emphasis is fixed on the process of change.

QUALITATIVE EVALUATION

In Chapter Eight we noted that qualitative methods help to describe the changes that a program produces. By so doing, qualitative methods accomplish several useful functions: (1) they help to rule out threats to internal validity; (2) they help describe how, who, and which particular elements of the program contribute to the results; and (3) they provide insight when programs do not produce the desired results.

One of the most important contributions that qualitative methods can make to program evaluation is that of testing the internal validity of an evaluation design. Remember that internal validity refers to the degree to which we may be certain that the program being evaluated, rather than other factors, caused the observed results. Internal validity is threatened when competing explanations for results cannot be ruled out.

In experimental designs most threats to internal validity are controlled by random assignment of subjects to groups. Sometimes, however, randomization is not possible or desirable. For instance, suppose you want to study the effect of television advertising on seat belt use in metropolitan areas. How can you randomly assign some people in a city to see the advertisements and others not? This is very difficult because of the broad and overlapping coverage of television stations. If randomization within a city will not work, an alternative is (on a random basis) to provide the messages in some cities and not in others. Such an approach is an improvement, but you would have to study a lot of cities to have a truly randomized design. A less expensive alternative would be to choose a few cities (perhaps as few as two) that are comparable by predetermined criteria, such as population, average income, economic base, climate and history concerning seat belt campaigns. Have television stations in half of the cities play the messages, while stations in the other half do not. Make sure the cities are far enough apart so that the TV stations playing the messages are not received in the control cities. Since we did not randomly select the cities, we have used a "quasi-experimental" design.

In "quasi-experimental" designs, individuals (or cities in our example) are not randomly selected and assigned to experimental and control conditions because randomization is not feasible for one reason or another. When using either true experimental or quasi-experimental designs, internal validity should not be assumed, it should be tested. In our example, one way to know that the control cities did not receive the messages is to do a case investigation. We may examine the logs of television stations to see if they played the commercials. We may survey people to see if they have seen the TV commercials. We may even interview the director of the local automobile safety association to find out what type of seat belt programs, if any, have been carried out in the past. This would ensure that the histories of the cities, in regards to seat belt campaigns, are known to the evaluators. If we can assume that all of the cities were comparable, and the messages were aired only in our experimental cities, then we might conclude that the people in the experimental cities increased their seat belt usage because of the messages. Once we are reasonably assured that the program has produced these desired results, we will want to describe how that result occurred. Qualitative methods are particularly useful for explaining how a health education intervention caused an observed result. By interviewing people as to why they buckle up, by asking people who have seen the TV spot how it altered their seat belt use, and by scanning the local newspapers or trade publications to see if articles have appeared that discuss the ad, the evaluator may gain insight into how and why the commercial may have worked.

Qualitative Evaluation and the Type III Error

Sometimes quantitative evaluations may indicate that the expected result is not evident. Say the seat belt ads had no effect. In such instances, qualitative methods may be useful in understanding why program expectations were not met. All too often the expected outcomes of a program do not occur because the program was never put into place. This occurrence is sometimes known as "Type III" error. Perhaps the commercials never played. Or, as is often the case with public service announcements, they played late at night when few people were awake to see them. In such instances, a Type III error has occurred because the program was never implemented as intended. By reviewing the TV station logs and by asking and observing at what time the ads were aired, the evaluator can determine whether the intervention failed to be implemented (A Type III error). An example of an actual case illustrates how qualitative methods were used to assess internal validity and to uncover a Type III error.

Methods for Qualitative Data Collection

In collecting qualitative data, the evaluator depends on four primary methods: observations, interviews, group techniques, and document or record searches. At first glance, you may notice that some of these techniques are also used in quantitative evaluations. Each of these methods range from a close-ended and preset format, to an open-ended and minimally structured format. Quantitative methods tend to use preset formats, while qualitative approaches are more open-ended. In general, it is good practice to use a combination of methods, both quantitative and qualitative. Also, the techniques you use should be determined by the scope of the project, funding, time available, access to data, and feasibility.

Participant Observation

Participant observation is the sine qua non of qualitative methods. Observation means that the evaluator spends time at the program sites in attempting to understand a program's context and dynamics. Observational techniques can range from non-participation, where the evaluator is a passive observer of events, to full participation, during which the evaluator partakes in all aspects of the program to "feel" its effects. As much as possible the evaluator should attempt to experience the program from the same perspective as program clients and staff. The participant observer wants to know what it is like being a client in the program: why people enter the program, how clients and staff interact, how each program component contributes to the overall outcome, what unplanned events occur, why they occur, what problems arise and why. Detailed description of people, events and reactions is the goal of the qualitative observer.

Interviews

The open-ended interview is the second most important method of qualitative data collection. We distinguish open-ended interviews from the range of more structured (and quantitative) interviews and questionnaires. Both open and close-ended interviews are administered by an interviewer, but the latter have a predetermined set of questions and choices of answers. There is an important difference between structured interviews and those in which the questions are not set, the answers are not predetermined, and the responses are recorded and transcribed verbatim. The main purpose of open-ended interviews is to collect information (data) that cannot be observed directly. Program elements that fall into this category include past events, how people feel, what they believe, and the meaning that they attribute to a program—all of which cannot be directly observed. These types of data become the grist for qualitative interviews, i.e., qualitative interviews tend to focus on history, feelings, beliefs, perceptions and behaviors which cannot be observed. Close-ended formats do not allow the informant enough "room" for a free-flowing expression of how the program is personally meaningful.

Sometimes an interview question appears to be open-ended but it really is close-ended because it suggests the answer in the question. For example, the question "How much did you learn from the program?" appears to be open-ended, but it really is not because it suggests an answer like "nothing," "a little," or "a lot." The question is merely a quantitative question with the response categories removed. A more genuinely open-ended question would be something like, "What did you learn from the program?" This question encourages the respondent to say what he thinks he learned from the program. It requires that the person answer in a sentence or a paragraph. Furthermore, the question itself does not suggest an answer, as the previous one did. It does, however, assume that the person did learn something from the program. Such assumptions are acceptable because the respondent always has the option of saying, "I didn't learn anything." The question also has the advantage of allowing follow-up questions, such as "What else do you think you learned as a result of participating in this program?"

Group Techniques

Group techniques, the third type of qualitative method for data collection, range from being highly structured to highly unstructured. A focus group is an example of a structured, yet open-ended (or "semi-structured") technique. As applied to program evaluation, focus groups are comprised of a small number of people (usually 4–8) with similar attributes (groups of program clients, program staff, or administrators, etc.). The group is interviewed as a collective by a facilitator who "focuses" on particular aspects of the program. The facilitator typically begins with a few predetermined questions. The participants are encouraged to interact freely while their responses are recorded (and later transcribed). The facilitator may ask additional questions depending on the nature of the group interaction. The advantage of focus groups is that they produce a large amount of evaluation data quickly and relatively inexpensively (compared to individual interviews).

While focus groups can be used at any stage of a program, i.e., before, during and after, the authors have had success in using focus groups of participants after the termination of several health education programs. In one case, we used focus groups with teenagers a year after they had participated in a program aimed at reducing teen pregnancy, smoking, and drug abuse. Each focus group had about seven teens and the questions mainly concerned how the program affected their behavior in these areas; questions also addressed recommendations these "graduates" had for improving the program. The focus groups produced a large amount of data that became an important part of the evaluation.

Program Documents

A document or record search is the fourth method of qualitative data collection. Every health education/health promotion program produces a huge "paper trail." There are almost always grant applications, program plans, annual reports, renewal applications, letters, educational materials, pamphlets and other written artifacts. These documents contain important information which can be used by the qualitative evaluator, including the program's philosophy, rationale and overall strategies. Such documents also include problem statements, goals and objectives, descriptions of intended target audiences, and descriptions of program interventions (as they were originally planned and as they were modified over time) and information about funding levels and staffing patterns. Documents reveal the history of a program, what it initially set out to accomplish, why certain decisions were made, what changes were made and why, and what the intended program processes and outcomes were at various stages of the program.

QUALITATIVE AND/OR QUANTITATIVE APPROACHES TO EVALUATION

As was mentioned in the previous chapter, the apparent dichotomy in approach to evaluation between the quantitative and qualitative actually goes to the very spirit and motivation for evaluation. Traditional (quantitative) evaluation is based on the tenets of the scientific method, where precision and consistency of measurement are paramount. These two qualities of measurement occupy their positions of importance because perhaps the most basic precept of the scientific method is that good research withstands replication. This means that not only must the conclusions of the original research emerge from the replication, but that the methods used must be as identical as possible. Precise, consistent measurement is borne of standard methods that are subject to a minimum of interpretation. Adherence to such standards produces findings that are precise, but (and this is the other side of the argument) often limited in scope to the point that the process that produced change is ignored altogether. If the point of evaluation is to determine the usefulness of the process in producing change, then **why** change occurred is at least as equally important as **how much** change occurred. Out of this debate, which has ebbed and flowed for decades, qualitative evaluation has emerged as a legitimate option.

CHOOSING THE BEST DESIGN FOR YOUR EVALUATION

Now that we've got some background in the principles that govern evaluation design, we need to sort out the details and figure out a pathway to guide us through the maze of decisions that are encountered in selecting an evaluation design. The basic steps that we need to consider are shown in Figure 9-12. As shown in the figure, there are four basic "macro" steps in developing evaluation designs: orientation, defining the problem, the basic design system and planning for data collection.

Step 1: Orientation

The first step in evaluation design is getting oriented to the situation. The program, the sponsors (those who are asking for the evaluation), the environment that the program operates within, the motivation for the program and the evaluation, and the population that is served by the program are all topics that need to be explored. It is crucial that you understand as much as you can about these issues before you do any thinking about design at all, because the information that you collect will probably rule out some designs and point you toward others. In addition, you will learn the resources that are at your disposal (personnel, time and money are the most important), the constraints that you must operate under, and the hidden agendas (unspoken goals) that may be present. The most important answers you need to get from the orientation phase of the evaluation design process are:

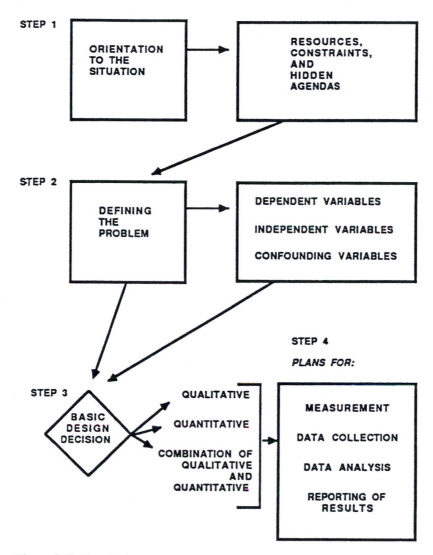

Figure 9-12. Four basic steps in selecting the best approach to evaluation design.

1. What is **expected** from the program?
2. What can be **observed** (that can be compared with what was expected)?

Step 2: Defining the Problem

This step in evaluation design is the most important because this is where you decide what you expect to evaluate. You might think that after spending time getting acquainted in step one that the evaluation problem would be obvious. The program operations and the structure of the evaluation sometimes coincide, but then again sometimes they seem at odds. Remember the discussion about the "focus of evaluation" at the end of the previous chapter? The basic idea presented was that programs can be evaluated on a number of different levels. Your own biases will lead you to "decide" which level of evaluation would be best for the program in question, but the sponsors of the evaluation may have another point of view. If you're like most health professionals, you probably feel that "effectiveness" should be part of most program evaluations. If this is true, then you'll be surprised to find out that in many cases those who order evaluation don't care as much about "effectiveness" as they do "meeting standards" or "efficiency."

When you've answered "What's to be evaluated?" then you can formulate some definitions to some basic terms.

1. **Independent Variables:** what the evaluation sponsors think makes the difference, if any, in the patients.
2. **Dependent Variables:** what the evaluation sponsors think will show the difference, if any, in the patients.
3. **Confounding Variables:** what you think could explain any difference found in the patients, other than the independent variable.

The definitions assigned to the three terms (above) will also give you a start toward deciding what information you will need to collect, how it can be collected, and from whom.

Step 3: Basic Design Decision

Once you have developed ideas about what is to be evaluated and have arrived at good definitions to the terms, you are ready to contemplate a decision about which "family" of designs to use. This is sort of like reaching a fork in the road with three options. One option is to use a qualitative approach and design the evaluation to use information from observations and other qualitative sources to describe what the program does, judge what does and doesn't work, and suggest reasons why. Another option is to use a quantitative approach. This traditional way of evaluating a program would involve measuring the dependent variable using an acceptable evaluation design, analyzing the data statistically and developing conclusions based on the results of the analysis. A third possibility is to combine qualitative and quantitative methods and try to incorporate the best features of each approach into the evaluation. In thinking about which route to take, ask yourself "What was expected from this program?" and "What can I observe (measure) that can be compared with the expected?" Are the expected and observed measurable or do they have to be described?

The decision about design is usually influenced by more than your own preferences and expertise. It's very common for the sponsors of the evaluation to have preconceived ideas of the way they would prefer evaluation to be carried out. Be sure to take time to understand their thinking about the approach to evaluation design, and try to convince them to change their mind if you think you have a better idea.

Step 4: Planning for Data Collection

The family of evaluation designs that you chose in the previous step—quantitative, qualitative or a combination of both—will lead you into this step naturally. If you are going to use a quantitative approach, then the requirements of those designs are straightforward. Control groups, valid and reliable measurement, and blinding of data collectors are all common features of quantitative designs that you may need to employ. Then you'll need to decide which design to use. Qualitative designs also have specific requirements, and you have to decide what would work best for your evaluation. If you want to combine quantitative and qualitative approaches, then you should balance the need for the structure and control that motivates quantitative designs with the need for sensitivity and description that is characteristic of the qualitative approach. Careful reading about the intricacies of the particular designs that might work well for you will guide you (see the readings at the end of this chapter).

Your decision about the design aside, you will always have to plan to actually carry out the evaluation. This subject is discussed in detail in the next chapter, but, as foreshadowing, the following list of tasks should be considered as part of the evaluation design process.

1. Plans for measurement: How will you measure the dependent variable? What about other "confounding" variables?
2. Plans for data collection: How will you collect the data? Will you need to use paper-and-pencil tests and, if so, where will you get the tests and the pencils? Will you have to organize a schedule to collect data or to provide a control group?
3. Plans for data analysis: Once you have collected the data, then

what will you do? Who will analyze the data and how will they do it? Are you collecting data that will allow the questions posed by the evaluation to be answered?

4. Plans for reporting results: How are the results to be reported? Do you have to produce a final report and submit it to administrators or others? Are you planning to publish the results in a professional journal? Will you have to present the results at a meeting and, if so, who might be the audience?

The final section of this chapter includes two reports of program evaluations. The examples are included not only to illustrate the steps in the evaluation process but also to demonstrate the compromises that are often necessary in arriving at approaches to evaluation that satisfy program managers, evaluation sponsors and evaluators. Two different formats have been used in structuring the examples. The format for the first example is structured to illustrate the correlation between the four steps in designing evaluation and the activities undertaken in evaluating the adolescent risk-reduction program. The format of the second example is organized to illustrate how the report of the evaluation results would appear.

EXAMPLE 1:
ADOLESCENT RISK–REDUCTION EDUCATION

This example illustrates the process and decisions needed in progressing through each of the four steps shown in Figure 9-12. The program was a federally funded health education program for adolescents. The program was intended to provide education about drugs, alcohol, tobacco and emotional health, with the purpose of "reducing risks." To implement the program, four sites were selected. Three used school systems and the other used a specific target community in an urban setting.

Step 1: Orientation

Interviews with the project coordinator and other key staff revealed that there were funds in the budget to hire evaluation personnel, evaluation was wanted and needed by the people in charge of the program, and that there weren't any volatile hidden agendas apparent at that point. The only constraint evident was that personnel hired were to be under the control of each site and not the project coordinator. This was seen as a possible source of concern for the future.

From the orientation, it was clear that the expectations of the program were that the knowledge and attitudes of the adolescents would improve such that they would not be as likely to engage in "risky" behaviors like drinking alcohol and smoking. It was learned that it would be possible to "observe" the knowledge and attitudes in the school settings in three of the four sites through the use of paper-and-pencil tests. The fourth site was not organized around schools, so the question of what to observe to compare with the expected was not addressed during the orientation phase.

Behavior change was an important goal for the project as a whole, as well as for each site. It wasn't selected as a main focus for the evaluation, though, because of the difficulty of measuring behavior in the adolescents across the sites. The potential problems were seen as barriers that could cripple effective measurement, so direct assessment of behavior was abandoned.

Step 2: Defining the Problem

It was clear that at least part of the evaluation for the program was to be dictated by the funding agency. The federal guidelines for the grant specified periodic reports of "activity" and "meeting standards." For the purposes of the health professionals working in the program, though, it was clear that the teaching program was to be evaluated. The dependent variables in three sites were to be knowledge and attitudes as revealed by periodic testing. In the community-based site the dependent variable was participation in the activities of the project, as measured by counting the continuing participants. The independent variables were clearly the novel programs provided by the grant. Possible confounding variables included other teaching that the students might be exposed to from the schools, churches or other community groups, as well as local attitudes toward adolescent drinking and smoking.

Step 3: Basic Design Decision

For three of the four sites the quantitative approach was selected. These were school-based programs that would operate within the schedules of the schools. Pretesting and posttesting seemed to make sense in the school environment, was attractive in terms of validity, and the project staff felt that the federal overseers were predisposed to quantitative evaluation. The school system policies precluded the use of any randomization, however. The qualitative approach was selected for the fourth, community-based site. The organization of the program seemed ideal for using qualitative methods, and the program staff felt that quantitative methods would be detrimental to program development.

Step 4: Planning for Data Collection

For the sites where quantitative evaluation was to be used, a before-and-after design with a control group was selected. Since the program budget could not support the teaching of all students at one time, the controls could be selected from those students not served. The qualitative site planned systematic observations of the adolescents in their community, a survey of non-participating adolescents in the community and extensive interviews of program participants.

The measurement of knowledge and attitudes in the quantitative sites was guided by dictates of the federal grant. Development and testing of instruments to measure knowledge and attitudes about alcohol and tobacco was planned.

Data were to be collected by the project staff at each site at predetermined times. Training programs were planned with the aim of standardizing the data collection procedures across the three school-based sites. The evaluation staff of the project were to direct the data collection. All completed instruments were to be sent to the project central office for processing. For the site with the qualitative evaluation, quarterly reports of evaluation activity were to be submitted to the project central office.

The analysis of the quantitative data was clear and straightforward. The goal was to determine the difference between the knowledge and attitudes at the pretest and the posttest. Statistical testing was to be used to determine the significance of any differences found. The qualitative data were to be analyzed by the project staff. They were to examine the data to look for themes describing the adolescents' reactions to the program, their behaviors and interactions, and other important reactions to the program activities.

The terms of the grant specified reporting procedures. In addition, the project central office staff planned semi-annual reports to all of the project staff where the progress and results of the evaluation would be presented. Any publishable results of the evaluation were to be submitted to the appropriate journals.

EXAMPLE 2: THE CASE OF PROJECT LIFE

Allan B. Steckler and Robert M. Goodman

The Problem

In 1983, the United Rubber, Cork, Linoleum, and Plastic Workers of America (a union), in cooperation with the School of Public Health of the University of North Carolina at Chapel Hill, received a three-year federal grant to develop a health promotion program for union members. The resulting program was named Project "LIFE," an acronym standing for "Labor and Industry Focus on Education." Because rubber workers have a high incidence of lung and other types of cancer, Project LIFE focused on cancer prevention in the workplace.

Two representatives from each of the thirteen experimental plants were trained in how to plan and conduct a model cancer control program. Trainers also provided their representatives with on-site consultation in their plants. The twelve control sites received neither the training nor the consultation. The consultants expected that as a result of the training and consultations, representatives would implement the model program in their respective plants.

Evaluation Design and Methods

To measure the effect of the program, an evaluation design was used similar to that shown in Figure 9-3, i.e., pretest/posttest with an experimental and control group. Questionnaires were mailed to workers to measure program outcomes for knowledge or behavior concerning workplace health threats; life-styles; workers' perceptions of the organizations in which they worked; needs-assessment program planning; and demographic questions (age, sex, etc.).

In addition to the quantitative measures, two types of qualitative evaluation data were collected: (1) in-depth case study of one plant that received the intervention; and (2) data which monitored the training activities and educational events that occurred at all experimental and control plants. These data included ongoing records of program planning activities, logs of the consultations, phone contacts, and correspondence between project staff and plant personnel.

Evaluation Results

The quantitative evaluation indicated that there were no significant changes between pretest and posttest in the experimental plants. That is, the quantitative study revealed no changes in knowledge, attitudes and behavior. Three explanations were suggested for the absence of program effects. The first two were threats to internal validity; they were externally occurring events over which Project LIFE personnel had no control. The third threat was a Type III error, i.e., a failure to implement the intervention.

The first threat was the implementation of the Occupational Safety and Health Administration's (OSHA) Hazard Communication Rule which went into effect during the Project LIFE study year. This rule required that plants that use hazardous chemicals educate workers about those chemicals. In the case study plant, the two Project LIFE representatives became involved in developing these required educational activities and they consumed all of their energies for six months. Earlier, we termed such outside influences on outcomes as history, a threat to internal validity.

The second threat to internal validity uncovered in the case study concerned the "turbulence" of the plant's environment. The rubber industry is a declining industry in the United States primarily because of competition from abroad. During the study year, there had been large layoffs in the rubber industry, and, in particular, the case study plant had been sold, which created a high degree of worry and concern among workers. As one worker said, "It's difficult to worry about life-style when you're worried about your job."

The third reason for no significant change concerned the minimal implementation of the principles for planning and conducting health promotion programs. These principles were taught in the training sessions and in the on-site consultation visits. For various reasons, the training and consultation visits were not implemented effectively; the new OSHA rule consumed the time of those who had been trained by Project LIFE, and many of those trained were either laid off or quit.

Without the monitoring and case study data, it is likely that the lack of significant changes in knowledge, attitudes, and behavior on the quantitative measures would have been attributed to the ineffectiveness of the health education principles, rather than to external factors such as history or turbulence, or that the principles were inadequately taught and implemented.

In this chapter we have presented the essentials of evaluation design. Read through the readings at the end for more detailed treatment of specific topics. You need to be aware that there are an enormous number of possibilities for evaluation design, but that their value hinges on appropriate measurement and control over the environment. Qualitative designs are somewhat more flexible than quantitative, measurement is focused on description rather than testing, and the conclusions from the evaluation are based on perceptions gleaned from the data rather than statistical testing.

READINGS

Campbell, D.T., and Stanley, J.C.: *Experimental and Quasi-Experimental Designs for Research.* Chicago, Rand McNally, 1963.

Cook, T.D., and Campbell, D.T.: *Quasi-Experimentation: Design & Analysis Issues for Field Settings.* Boston, Houghton Mifflin, 1979.

Fisher, R.A.: *Statistical Methods for Research Workers,* 14th ed. New York, Hafner, 1970.

Gilmore, G.D., Campbell, M.D., and Becker, B.L.: *Needs Assessment Strategies for Health Education and Health Promotion.* Dubuque, IA, Brown & Benchmark, 1989.

Kosecoff, J., and Fink, A.: *Evaluation Basics: A Practitioner's Manual.* Beverly Hills, Sage, 1982.

Levy, P.S., and Lemeshow, S.: *Sampling for Health Professionals.* Belmont, CA, Lifetime Learning, 1980.

Patton, M.Q.: *Practical Evaluation.* Beverly Hills, Sage, 1982.

Patton, M.Q.: *Qualitative Evaluation Methods.* Beverly Hills, Sage, 1980.

Rossi, P.H., Freeman, H.E., and Wright, S.R.: *Evaluation: A Systematic Approach.* Beverly Hills, Sage, 1979.

Sarvela, P.D., and McDermott, R.J.: *Health Education Evaluation and Measurement: A Practitioner's Perspective.* Dubuque, IA, Brown & Benchmark, 1993.

Chapter Ten

DATA COLLECTION AND ANALYSIS

The previous chapter dealt with the issues and methods for designing program evaluation. Designs for evaluation are really plans for data collection, but selecting a design raises many more questions. This chapter will help to answer those questions by discussing collection and analysis of program evaluation data.

To do a good job of collecting and analyzing data, you must plan with religious zeal. Zeal is necessary because, in most cases, you only get one chance to collect the data needed for evaluation. If the analysis shows that additional information is needed, it is usually too expensive and time consuming to go back and collect what's needed. Taking extra time to thoroughly plan evaluation, including detailed descriptions of how information will be collected and analyzed, will pay off when the final report is written.

BASIC PRINCIPLES

Planning for data collection and analysis involves two fundamental considerations. The first involves the collection process and includes the type of data to be collected, the way it is to be collected, who will be collecting it from whom, the setting for data collection, how long it will take to collect all the data you need from the average, the speediest and the slowest subject, and what else will be going on with the subjects and the setting while you're trying to collect data. The second consideration is less complicated but no less important: How will the data get from collection to the final report? What analyses will be done? Will the analysis be done by hand or using a computer? If the computer is in the picture, then you can save yourself endless screaming, hair-pulling and perhaps violence by carefully considering what's involved with getting the data into the machine and getting the answers out that you want.

Never, but never make the mistake of assuming that the computer is smarter than you are or that it can always finish what you have started.

You have to know precisely what goes into the computer in order to be able to make sense of what comes out. If you're not a computer person but will need to use computers for your evaluation, then get to know a competent source of help, preferably the one that will be analyzing your data. Communicate very clearly with this individual, or group, and develop a good working relationship.

Consistency

One more data collection and analysis topic that deserves special attention is consistency. Strive to be consistent in everything you do in collecting and analyzing your data. Try to treat every individual or group the same way; give them the same instructions to the letter, if possible. This practice will help reduce non-systematic error. For example, if you are using a questionnaire to collect your data, then the instructions that you give people should be uniform. If you help some people with interpreting items but are too busy to help others that have the same questions, then you have non-systematic error creeping into the data. You'll never be able to find it, and you wouldn't know how to fix it if you could find it. Treat everyone alike. Give everyone the same instructions. Provide the same amount of assistance to everyone. And, if you have to deviate from your planned data collection procedures, then keep excruciatingly detailed records of your deviations. Write down (right now) what you changed, why, for whom, and whether you're going to have this be a one-time change or a permanent change in procedures. Mark the data forms where the change occurred. The basic rules are simple: be consistent and document any changes that you make. Don't trust your memory.

Evaluation Instruments

The instruments that you use to collect data for program evaluation should be treated like mechanics' tools. To have them work properly you have to understand how to use them and what can go wrong. The best way to become familiar with the instruments is to administer them several times before using them in the evaluation. This "pilot testing" will help you to learn how to get the best results from the instruments. If you have just spent a lot of time developing them, then the pilot testing isn't necessary, of course. If it's been a while since you last collected data or if the population or program has changed, then you are well advised to do some pilot work.

Subjects of Evaluation

As with the instruments that are used to collect evaluation data, you need to be familiar with the people that will provide the data. You need to be clear in your understanding of how the people will react both to the fact that you are trying to get information from them as well as to the method that you're using. Literacy and familiarity with specific terms are pretty obvious potential problems, but there can also be more subtle factors that people are sensitive about. In most cases they will react by not giving you the information that you want and need. On the other hand, if people know that you're collecting information that will be used for evaluation, they may take the opportunity to show their respect for you by praising you when you don't deserve it, or vent their frustrations and distort the information that they provide. Either way, you haven't gotten the information you need. To avoid these irritations, get to know your subjects. Find out if you will be asking sensitive questions, and if you are and can't figure a way around them, then try to design an approach that will at least change unsystematic into systematic error.

Such issues as literacy and specialized terminology are not trivial concerns, by the way. Pilot testing the instruments should tell you if you're likely to have problems with people not understanding, and often as not, you'll end up changing the instruments to make them simpler and clearer.

Considerations About the Setting for Data Collection

The instruments that you use to collect evaluation data are important, the subjects that will provide the data are important, and the setting in which the actual data collection takes place is also important. Remember that we're striving for consistency and clear communication in data collection. We want to be able to treat each subject the same and to have all the subjects react to our efforts in the same way. We want everyone to understand what they're being asked to do, how to fill out the question-naires, and what we mean by all the terms. To make these hopes come true, we need to have an environment that is reasonably consistent. Ideally, we would like an environment that is free of distractions, quiet and private, and pretty much under our control. This almost never occurs in real life, however, so evaluation usually has to take place within the usual activities of the organization. Select the environment for evaluation activities so that you will have a consistent level of interruptions and distractions. Don't end up with the situation where you have turbulence with some subjects and not with others.

Collection Data with Analysis (by Computer) in Mind

As time has passed, our society has evolved from one where most individuals and organizations processed information manually, to one that used "large" computers for record keeping (like the payroll for large companies or students' grades at many universities), to one that now uses both large and small computers for record keeping, research applications, and for lots of everyday things. As this progression in technology has occurred, the techniques for evaluation have also evolved. Today, most people have access to computers and don't have to analyze their data by hand. Some still do, though, mainly because they don't understand the machines, they don't trust them, or whatever. Whether you're enthusiastic, afraid, distrustful, or generally alienated from computer technology, it makes sense to be able to talk to a person who will be doing your computer analysis. To begin, there are two different aspects of computer analysis that you need to keep straight. One involves putting the information that you want to analyze into the computer, "data entry" in computerese. This part of the process is very different from using the computer to analyze the data but is intimately connected nevertheless. The second aspect is the analysis of data.

Putting information into the computer so that it can be processed to get out the answers you want requires translating what you collect into a form that the machine can work with. This "form" can use numbers, letters or both, but the essence of the process is translating the information that has been collected into language that the machine can work with. Your task as the evaluator who wants her/his data analyzed is to figure out a way to do this—or work with someone who's going to do it for you. If you have used scales or tests that can be scored, then this is usually easy. If you've collected data that don't translate as easily, then you have to figure out a way to do it because the computer can only deal with information that it can recognize and manipulate. In addition to the data that is directly involved with the evaluation, there is crucial information that describes important things about the subjects, the program, and other relevant factors that may influence the evaluation. You have to decide how much of this information you need and then translate that as well.

The second part of computer processing is data analysis. Assuming that your data are in the machine in the proper form, this part of analysis is like ordering food in a restaurant. You order what you want from the data and the computer provides it. However, the decisions about the type of analysis to order may be challenging.

QUANTITATIVE DATA ANALYSIS

Data analysis is the most anxiety-provoking part of evaluation for many people. If you can remember one basic concept, a lot of the mystery of analysis will disappear: **Is what was observed different from what was expected?** Don't be put off by the informality of this statement. Strange as it may seem, the conceptual basis of nearly all evaluation and statistics comes from this question.

The first question that we have to answer is what we mean by "expected?" Expectations come from intentions; intentions are spelled out by objectives or constructs. Program objectives are really statements of intention, so they spell out expectations; it's as simple as that. If the objectives are not clearly spelled out, then you'll have trouble determining what "expected" means, but then you'll also have trouble with all other phases of the evaluation. When the expected results of the program are clear, one of three basic analysis questions becomes apparent:

  a. Is what we observed different from the standards of performance that we would predict?
  b. Is what we observed after our intervention different from what we observed before our intervention?
  c. Is what we observed consistent with a trend that we would predict?

These three questions are basic. There are variations, of course, but if you can reduce the essential purpose of your evaluation to answering one of these questions, the analysis of data will be much easier. Reducing the essential purpose of the evaluation to answering one of the above questions leads into consideration of exactly how the question will be answered.

Basic Steps in Data Analysis

Just thinking about data analysis can be a hair-raising experience for some people. Such anxiety is more common than you might think, but it can be helped by organization. We can organize this task into the following steps:

1. Summarize data from all measures both descriptive and quantitative;
2. Classify quantitative measures into groups according to the relevant descriptive categories—by sex, race, age, and program participation, for example;
3. Identify nominal, ordinal, interval and ratio scale data and be sure that the analysis you want to carry out is appropriate for the scale of data;
4. Inspect or statistically test for differences;
5. Draw tentative conclusions based on testing and/or inspection; and
6. Think about competing explanations for findings and re-analyze the data if necessary.

The first consideration is measurement. Most evaluations include collection of data of several types. Descriptive information includes data that describe the program participants: their age, sex, ethnic group, etc. Quantitative information is the data that measures knowledge, attitudes, behaviors, and the like. We typically use the quantitative data to answer our basic question in conjunction with the descriptors of the population. Some evaluations do not collect any quantitative information, though. The point behind recognition of the type of data collected is that the type dictates the analysis. Descriptive data are very useful for counting and describing the program participants but usually cannot be used to express their knowledge or attitudes. Quantitative data are precisely for expressing things that we can measure. Keep these two types of information separate in your mind; think of descriptive data as ways of classifying the program participants and the quantitative data as ways of measuring their experience in the program. Put another way, quantitative data may allow us to make inferences about the effects of the program, descriptive data may allow us to classify program effects. Let's look at a short example.

Suppose we were evaluating the effectiveness of an innovative family planning clinic for teenagers, using the rate of unplanned pregnancy among teenage women in our community as the dependent variable. Our method of data collection might be to interview the pregnant women, where we would collect information about their family background, previous pregnancies, and experience with "our" family planning clinic. The rate of unplanned pregnancy could only serve as a measure of the effectiveness of our clinic if we had something to use for comparison. The descriptive data on experience with "our" clinic would enable us to create such a comparison. We could classify the teenage women according to their participation in our program and determine whether the rates of unplanned pregnancy were different for those who had and had not participated. Notice that in this example we are basing our analysis on question "a" above. That is, the services of our innovative family planning clinic provide us with standards of performance that we expect to observe in the teenage women served. In essence, we expect those we serve to have less unplanned pregnancies than similar women not served. By interviewing all the pregnant teenagers that we can find, we would be able to create two categories: those who had been served by the program and those who had not. If our program was successful, we would expect to find that most, if not all, of the pregnant teens had **not** been served by our clinic. The descriptive information about family background and previous pregnancies might help us to create other subgroups that could help to describe and explain the findings. For example, we might find that among those who had been to our clinic that very few had had previous pregnancies. Or we might find that those with unstable family backgrounds were most likely to use our clinic. See the point? The descriptive data allows us to classify the teens into groups that help to further our understanding of the clinic and teenage pregnancy.

Classification of Data

Classification of the information that we have collected into groups and subgroups allows us to proceed with the analysis to a point where we can generate some tentative answers to the questions that prompted the evaluation in the first place. Sometimes just classifying the facts will give you enough information to answer the questions to your satisfaction by inspection. (That's right, just looking at the categories.) If so, then count yourself lucky and go home early! If inspection doesn't give a clear enough picture or if the people you work for want/need a clear picture and accompanying numbers, then you still have work to do.

Statistical Analysis

As we said before, statistical analysis is based on the idea of trying to determine whether what you observe is really different from what was expected. Figuring out how to calculate statistics is no mean feat, so the first thing to consider is whether you should get help or not, and if so, what type. Begin by asking about basic data types, typical questions to be answered, and statistics commonly used. Whether you figure out the results yourself or get help from a consultant, statistical testing will provide you with information about the relationships among the categories of information that goes beyond what you can see (inspect). Sometimes statistical testing simply confirms what is already apparent, but in other cases it adds new information. Whether you have relied on inspection or statistics, you now have the information that should allow you to answer the basic evaluation questions and draw some conclusions.

Conclusions from Analysis

Conclusions are the formal answers to questions that stimulated the evaluation. Was the program effective? Are patients processed efficiently? Does the staff perform their duties at reasonable minimal standards? Has the problem been solved by the program? Are patients served any better now than before the program was in effect? Drawing conclusions must be carried out with care because by necessity they involve "sticking your neck out." Sometimes the data are so conclusive themselves that a formal statement is obvious and unnecessary, but in many cases, the conclusions will not be obvious. Nevertheless, conclusions are a necessary capstone for evaluations.

COMPROMISE AND COMPETING EXPLANATIONS

Nearly all program evaluations require compromise in measurement, design, data collection, and so on. Like we've pointed out in previous chapters, compromise is not good or bad, it's a fact of life. Fact of life or not, compromise means that the results of the evaluation are based on grounds that may not be firm in all places. This is not something to get overly defensive about though, because all evaluations involve compromise, and the difference between compromises that invalidate the results and those that just cause you to sigh with regret is not always clear. Regardless, you have to look at the results of evaluation with the compromises in mind and think to yourself, "Are there other explanations for the results that are just as good as the reasons given?" In other words, are there reasonable competing explanations for the results, other than "the program caused the change?" Reviewing the latter parts of Chapter Nine where we discussed design, you will find several limitations on internal and external validity. Is there evidence of these limitations? Is there any way that you can estimate their effect? Could they have contributed to, or totally caused, the results? Are you sure that your data were measuring what you wanted? Are you sure that the effects you measured were due to the program and not some other influence? You'll probably find that answering these questions is both challenging and sobering. The questions can be sobering because they're critical of something that took up a lot of your time and brainpower; challenging because many of the answers have to be "I don't know."

Collecting data without letting subtle biases creep in and carrying out analysis to figure out what the data can tell you are tasks that can stress out a Zen master. Consistency and control are the key words to remember. Treat every subject alike when you collect data; be sure that the environment is controlled as much as possible to preserve consistency.

QUALITATIVE DATA ANALYSIS

The methods used for qualitative evaluation were surveyed in Chapter Nine. Once the evaluator has used several methods to collect a wealth of qualitative data about a program, then he/she must next distill the raw data into a meaningful and clear statement of program accomplishment. Such a statement is produced by analyzing the qualitative data which was collected. Qualitative data analysis usually proceeds through the following steps: (1) organizing the data, (2) coding, (3) developing patterns, (4) developing typologies, and (5) developing flow diagrams. Each of these data analysis steps is briefly described below, and a special analytic technique, the case study, is also explained.

Organizing the Data

Qualitative data collection usually produces volumes of data to be analyzed. The first step in data analysis, therefore, is to check that all the data is collected and if possible to fill in missing data. Be especially certain that the transcriptions of interviews are accurate and are in the words of the people interviewed. Sometimes individuals who transcribe interviews like to "fix" what people say so that it is grammatically correct. By keeping text in the original language a more accurate depiction of the program is achieved. Therefore, the evaluator wants direct quotes, not grammatically correct text.

After all the data has been checked and corrected and missing data filled in, then at least one extra copy of the data should be made and put away in a safe place. Many evaluators have horror stories to tell about losing their hard-earned data and not being able to replace it. In fact, many evaluators make two copies of their data: one is put away and two for analysis.

Coding Qualitative Data

The next step is the coding of the data. Coding is a process in which the evaluator reads all the observation notes, transcripts of interviews and group techniques, and all of the collected program documents. When reading through these materials, the evaluator looks for text that illustrates key points or ideas. These key points or ideas are coded in the margin of the text using a coding scheme developed by the evaluator. Coding can take many forms and books are available that teach the technique. (See readings by Patton and Miles for further information.) The evaluator should choose a coding scheme that best fits the evaluator's style. It is common practice in coding qualitative data to have it done by two independent coders as a way of increasing reliability.

Looking for Patterns

The purpose of qualitative analysis is to inductively find patterns in the evaluation data. To find such patterns, the next step in qualitative data analysis is to organize the coded data into categories. To accomplish this, the evaluator organizes each text of coded data by the same code. For instance, if the evaluator asked how a program was beneficial, each passage of text coded as an example of a program benefit is extracted and placed with other such examples. Once the data are organized by like codes, categories of results become evident. For example, a number of clients might say that a program benefited them in a particular way. These categories then become the inductively derived patterns which are the basic qualitative results.

Developing Typologies

The fourth step of qualitative analysis is to organize patterns into typologies. As Patton explains, "Typologies are classification systems made up of categories that divide some aspect of the world into parts." There are two types of typologies: indigenous and evaluator created. The former type uses categories that are used by the people being studied. The latter type are created by the evaluator as a result of data analysis. For example, high school students often have terms for different categories of students, e.g., "jocks," "preppies," "nerds," "freaks," etc. An evaluator studying high schools might explain these indigenous typologies and then use them to show which category of students most (or least) benefited from the program being studied. Program benefits could be placed in categories developed by the evaluator. For instance, categories of benefits might be increased knowledge, increased skill, increased appreciation, or increased support gained for a program. The coding scheme for benefits helps the evaluator determine what categories are appropriate.

As an illustration of the use of coding schemes, consider the case of a federally sponsored health promotion program implemented in 27 different sites. The sites were spread around the country. The evaluation suggested that there were two broad categories of sites which we labeled "logo" and "non-logo" sites. The logo sites had developed logos for their programs which symbolized their active, energetic programs that highly identified with the federal sponsoring agency. The non-logo sites used some of the methods and data provided by the federal sponsoring agency, but they did not strongly identify with the agency's overall program — they tended to maintain their local organization's identity and as a result they did not develop special "logos" for the federally sponsored program. This evaluator-developed typology became important to the federal sponsoring agency (the evaluation client), because they realized first that they had assumed that all sites were "logo" sites and, second, that the "non-logo" approach was valid and effective and one that they should support.

Developing Flow Diagrams

Since qualitative methods usually focus on program processes, i.e., what occurred, when things occurred, who was involved, etc., they can be used to develop flow diagrams of a program. An important data analytic technique, therefore, is to use qualitative data to construct a diagram of how a program actually operated. Such a diagram could include the key steps or components of a program, what occurred first, second, and so on. Such diagrams are very useful in illustrating what the key components of a program were and of giving an overall perspective of a program.

Inductively derived flow diagrams can be compared to flow diagrams that depict how the program was supposed to operate. Most programs have either an implicit or explicit sequence or series of steps or events which are supposed to occur. Therefore, qualitative evaluators often construct and compare two flow diagrams: one depicting how the program was supposed to operate or occur (known as the presumptive or expected diagram), and the other showing how it actually operated (the actual diagram). The differences between the two are then used to help explain the evaluation findings. For instance, assume that a program did not produce much of an effect, and in comparing the expected flow diagram with the actual diagram, the evaluator determines that a key component of the program did not occur. This would then suggest why the program did not have the intended results.

REPORTING ON CASE STUDIES

Case studies represent a special form of qualitative data analysis. In conducting one or more case studies, an evaluator would likely use data collection methods such as participant observations, open-ended interviews, focus groups, and content analysis of program documents. What distinguishes a case study, however, is in how the unit of analysis is defined and the depth with which that unit of analysis is investigated. "Unit of analysis" is a research term which is used to define what it is that is being studied. In program evaluations, units of analysis can be individual people, subgroups of people (such as boys and girls), decisions, programs or particular parts of programs, or organizations.

In health education/health promotion evaluation studies, a common type of case study is one in which a program is operating in a number of sites (such as a curriculum being taught in several schools) and an in-depth evaluation (i.e., a case study) is done in one of those sites. Like qualitative methods in general, the purpose of case studies is to understand in depth how and why things happened the way they did. A case study, however, focuses on only one site or one organization or one component of a program. If conducting an evaluation of a program is like putting that program under a microscope, then a case study is like increasing the power of the microscope's lens. In Chapter Eight, an example was given in which one of the 23 Project LIFE sites was used for an in-depth case study. The results of that case study proved to be very useful in helping explain why the program did not work the way it was intended to work.

Data analysis, quantitative and qualitative, is as much art as science. The basic guidelines set forth in this chapter are intended to nudge you toward looking at the data in a consistent, logical fashion. The primary task in data analysis, though, is to answer the questions that motivated the evaluation in the first place.

We have emphasized that it is good evaluation practice to use both quantitative and qualitative methods where possible. Yet, such a combination of methods is not easy, because qualitative and quantitative data differ in the ways they are collected and analyzed. In using quantitative methods, the evaluator places a premium on the consistency with which instruments like questionnaires and surveys are designed and applied. Questionnaires and surveys are examples of "technologies as instruments," where the evaluator is removed from the sources of data. In qualitative data collection, the evaluator (you) is the instrument. The following example illustrates how quantitative and qualitative methods can be combined to provide a better evaluation than either method could provide alone.

EXAMPLE: EVALUATION OF THE TRAINING WORKSHOP ON PLANNING AND MANAGEMENT OF HEALTH EDUCATION COMPONENTS OF "COMBATING CHILDHOOD COMMUNICABLE DISEASE"

Allan B. Steckler and Robert M. Goodman

The Problem

Many African countries suffer from high rates of infant and childhood deaths due to diarrheal diseases, and from communicable diseases which can be prevented by immunizations. The prevention of such diseases has strong behavioral, and thus, health education components. Yet, many people in Africa who hold health education positions have not had much formal training in health education. Therefore, several governments in

Africa decided to enlist the help of U.S. governmental health agencies in conducting a month-long training program. The program was for those health educators who worked in "Combatting Childhood Communicable Disease" (CCCD) programs and the managers who operated such programs. The goals of the training program were to improve the educators' and managers' abilities to plan, conduct and evaluate community health education programs.

The Training Program

The training workshop, which was held in Nigeria, consisted of four main phases, each of which lasted approximately one week: (1) a participatory needs-assessment and workshop planning phase; (2) a content/information phase (i.e., a teaching phase); (3) a health education plan development phase; and (4) a plan presentation, critiquing and rewriting phase. The program sponsors anticipated that the training workshop would be conducted a number of times in order to reach health educators in as many African countries as possible. Therefore, the workshop had to be evaluated so that its strengths and weaknesses would be identified and thus it could be improved. An extensive evaluation was conducted that employed both quantitative and qualitative methods. Each of these methods is briefly described below.

The Evaluation

Needs-Assessment Questionnaire (Quantitative). Prior to the training program, all of the health educators and program managers who worked in the countries to be represented at the workshop were given a needs-assessment questionnaire. The questionnaire asked about competencies and skills of health educators and about the quality of the working relationships between health educators and program managers. The results of the needs assessment were used to help plan the workshop.

Knowledge Test (Qualitative/quantitative). All of the workshop participants were given an essay-type knowledge test before and immediately after the workshop. The test concerned knowledge about health education program planning and relationships between health educators and program managers. The essay tests were graded using specific scoring criteria, so that the qualitative answers were eventually given quantitative scores.

Attitude/Self-Efficacy Test (Quantitative). This close-ended test measured participants' attitudes towards the value of health education. It also measured whether health educators felt that they were capable of planning and implementing health education plans (i.e., self-efficacy).

Participant Observations (Qualitative). Workshop evaluators kept a daily journal of workshop activities including who participated, what problems arose, and how participants and staff reacted to each other. The main goal of the participant observations was to create a written record of precisely what happened each day of the workshop and why things happened the way that they did.

Focus Group (Qualitative). At the end of the workshop, a focus group was conducted with six participants. In one hour, the group addressed several open-ended questions pertaining to the strengths and weaknesses of the workshop. The focus group was conducted jointly by two evaluators who both recorded what was said. Immediately after the focus group, the two evaluators compared their notes to ensure that they agreed on the main ideas revealed in the session.

Analysis of Health Education Plans (Quantitative). The participants had worked in teams by country, each team producing a health education plan. After the workshop, the plans were analyzed by the evaluators who used a specific, quantitative scoring method which graded each plan.

Participants' Rating Form (Qualitative and Quantitative). A questionnaire with both open-ended and close-ended questions was given to participants at the end of the workshop. The questionnaire asked the participants to rate or comment about various aspects of the workshop, such as the lectures, the facilities, the workshop's strengths and weaknesses, and suggestions for improvement.

Data Analysis and Results

Once all the evaluation data had been collected, the evaluators analyzed separately the data obtained from each method. The quantitative data were analyzed using standard statistical techniques. The qualitative data were analyzed using the methods described in this chapter: the data were coded, and patterns, typologies and flow diagrams were developed.

The results from each source of data (needs-assessment questionnaire, knowledge test, etc.) became a brief chapter in a written evaluation report. Once each source of data was analyzed separately, the evaluators searched for findings that were common across several sources of data. These common findings were included in the final chapter of the report and represented the main findings. The main findings were then used to make recommendations for future workshops.

READINGS

Cochran, W.G.: *Planning and Analysis of Observational Studies.* New York, Wiley, 1983.

Isaac, S., and Michael, W.B.: *Handbook in Research and Evaluation.* San Diego, EdITS, 1981.

Patton, M.Q.: *Qualitative Evaluation.* Beverly Hills, Sage, 1980.

Miles, M.B., and Huberman, A.M.: *Qualitative Data Analysis.* Beverly Hills, Sage, 1984.

Chapter Eleven

PRESENTING THE RESULTS OF EVALUATION

In this chapter we will cover some basic principles that can help you to put your best foot forward in presenting the results of evaluation. The discussion of this issue will be divided into three main topics: identifying important characteristics and desires of the audience, addressing the purposes of the evaluation, and techniques of presentation. A good evaluation report should, first and foremost, answer the questions that the evaluation was supposed to answer (or make it clear why not), as well as present the results in a form that is appropriate for the audience/sponsors of the evaluation.

MAKING YOUR REPORT FIT THE AUDIENCE

To be effective, evaluation reports should be written to communicate clearly with the audience. Clear communication is dependent on your knowing what the audience needs to know as well as how to get the message across. What you need to communicate are the evaluation results, but you have to find out about the audience to learn how to present the results most effectively. A useful first step in finding out how to present your results is to orient your point of view toward thinking of the people that will read your report as "consumers." If you play the part of the producer and think of the audience as the consumers, then the first thing you need to do to sell your product is find out as much as you can about their consumer behaviors. (You may already know some things about the consumers from doing the evaluation, but be aware that they may show a different face when they become consumers of the results.) There are two main categories of questions that you will need to answer if you are to match your report with the audience: personal characteristics of the audience and their connections to the results of the evaluation.

Audience Characteristics

You may think it strange to learn that you should be interested in the personal characteristics of the audience of an evaluation report. The point is that you need to learn enough to make a good guess about how your audience is going to receive the results of the evaluation. Are they likely to take in the results without preconceived ideas, or do they have expectations about what the evaluation was supposed to show? You can begin improving your understanding of the audience by getting answers to the following questions:

1. About the Audience:
    a. Who are they? How many are there? What are their ages, sexes, ethnic backgrounds, occupations and hobbies?
    b. Are there any particular issues that they are sensitive about?
    c. What are their areas and levels of expertise, both personally and professionally?
2. About the Audience's Connection to the Evaluation: In what ways is the audience connected to the evaluation?
    a. Do they have any biases or hidden agendas (unspoken goals) about the program or the evaluation?
    b. What are their options for action based on the results of the evaluation?

The answers to these questions will be invaluable to you in writing your report. Perhaps the most important things that you should be able to glean from collecting this information are the following:

1. **The style of writing you should use.**
    a. What should be your level of language? How can you communicate clearly and avoid "talking down" to the audience or missing them with technical language?
    b. Should you write your report in the context of larger issues that are important to the audience, or should you stay strictly to the point and be brief?
2. **The level of detail you should use.**
    a. Should you emphasize the technical aspects of the evaluation or barely mention data collection and analysis?
    b. Should you carefully explain all the assumptions that you made in choosing the instruments and methods for analysis, or should you emphasize the results?

3. **Specific results that the audience is looking for or does not want to see.**
    a. Are there ethical or legal questions raised by the results? If so, what do you think your role should be in dealing with them as an evaluator?
    b. Is your point of view different than the sponsors of the evaluation, employees of the program or the audience of the report?

MAKING YOUR POINT

Do not, repeat, do not forget that the purpose of evaluation is to get answers to specific questions. Amazingly enough, many evaluation reports never address the basic questions that they set out to answer. Don't let yourself become so fixated on the intricacies of data collection or analysis that you forget to specifically address the reasons that the evaluation was done in the first place. But what happens when the results of the evaluation aren't clear? The best thing to do is to openly acknowledge the fact that the answer isn't clear (Still? After all the time and money spent on the evaluation?), and carefully and judiciously speculate on what would be needed to clear it up.

PRESENTING THE RESULTS OF EVALUATION

There are no "commandments" for presenting results of evaluations, but what has developed into tradition over time is what we'll call the "article format." The article format is the format that is used for publishing results of most research. The report is divided roughly into sections beginning with an introduction, followed by a methods section, results, conclusions, and sometimes a discussion.

Introduction

The introduction should introduce the report of the results in the context of the evaluation project. The most extensive part of the introduction should be the description of the program that was evaluated. Briefly discuss the history of the program and, in more detail, its objectives and methods of operation. Be sure to include enough detail in your description of the program to allow the reader to be able to interpret the results of the evaluation. At the end of the introduction, include a specific statement outlining what you thought the job of the evaluator was, and briefly describe the approach taken to carry out the task of evaluation.

Methods

The methods section of the report tends to be technical. It is the section that describes how the evaluation was structured, the instruments that were used, data collection, and analysis. What goes into this section depends on the characteristics of the audience. Naturally, this section tends to be longer and more detailed for technically sophisticated audiences. For non-technical audiences, critique this section carefully to avoid use of terms and language that would cause confusion. Be sure to define any technical terms or professional jargon that you think might be foreign to the audience. It is usually a good idea to prepare an appendix that includes a complete exposition of all methods used in instrument testing, data collection and analysis.

Results

The results are the central focus of the report. Make every effort possible to present the results clearly. Avoid lengthy statements cataloging the responses to each questionnaire item. Graphs and illustrations are usually very helpful and, when well-prepared, can effectively summarize large amounts of information very efficiently. Organize the results in a way that highlights the basic questions asked by the evaluation, and include detailed findings under each question.

Conclusions

The conclusions that you draw from the evaluation are probably what readers will remember most. Conclusions are formal statements of the answers to the basic questions asked by the evaluation. For example, an evaluation designed to determine the efficiency of a program would report results of measuring program input and output but would conclude with a statement about efficiency. The results might also provide the detail about which aspects of the operation were most and least efficient. Because they tend to be remembered and because they are simple statements of answers to questions that are often complicated, drawing conclusions can be serious business, not something for the faint of heart.

Discussion

A final section discussing the evaluation as a whole may be added after the results. You may decide to add such a section when there are comments that should be made, but they don't fit into the other parts of the report. Specifically, the comments may relate to alternative explanations for the results of the evaluation, and implication of the conclusions. You may recall in Chapter Nine, we discussed several limitations to internal and external validity. When you suspect that your results may indeed have been compromised by some of these forces, your suspicions should be made clear, but only as possible competing explanations for the results of the evaluation. For example, if you think that the chronic disease clinic that you evaluated saw more patients because of a television program dramatizing heart disease instead of the new publicity that the clinic introduced, but you cannot be sure, then this final section is a good place to discuss that possibility. Other types of comments that find their way into the discussion section of many reports are implications of the conclusions of the evaluation, suggestions for correcting problems with the program that came to light during the evaluation, and sometimes references to political or administrative forces that influenced the evaluation.

ILLUSTRATING EVALUATION RESULTS

There are many ways that can be used to illustrate the results of evaluation. (Since our purpose here is to introduce you to the important concepts, further reading about the details of the techniques may be helpful to you. Consult the readings listed at the end of this chapter.) Of course, the first choice that you have is to simply write down all the data that you collected and let them speak for themselves in the results section of your report. This could take a lot of time and space, though, and most readers don't want to have to wade through all the data and figure out the results of the evaluation themselves. Most readers prefer to have the data summarized and displayed in such a way that the results of the evaluation are clearly shown. There are essentially two different methods that you can use to display results: tables and figures. Before we deal with the particulars, some general comments about using tables and figures are needed:

1. Tables and figures should summarize and illustrate accurately and clearly.
2. Label tables and figures completely.
3. Design tables and figures in the context of the report to help communication.
4. Scales should be consistent and non-distorting.
5. Simple is best.

Tables and figures are only worthwhile when they display information accurately and clearly.* We use them to present information in a compact way, so the more information "compacted" in a table or figure, the greater the economy. But if we compact information to the point that we lose accuracy or sacrifice clarity, the economy is false.

Accuracy

Accuracy is at least partly dependent on the amount of information that is included in tables and figures, with more information generally meaning greater accuracy. But it is clear that too much information leads to a cluttered mess and defeats the purpose of the display altogether. This realization leads us to a dilemma in trying to figure out how much information to include. We need to find a point where we have included enough data to give us the most accuracy, but not so much that we lose clarity. You have to be the judge of accuracy and clarity, based on what you want to convey in the display as well as what you know about the audience who will read the report.

Labels

Every table and figure needs to be labeled completely. There should be no doubt in the readers' minds as to what is being shown, to what group it refers, what was measured and how, and when the data were collected. The test of proper labeling is to be able to remove the table or

---

*See Wainer (1984) in the readings at the end of this chapter.

figure from the report and still be able to identify it and understand what is being shown.

Context

Tables, and especially figures (charts and graphs), should be used to summarize and illustrate important points about the evaluation. They shouldn't repeat what has been explained in the text, but they should present information in the context of the report. You can help the reader to make the connection between figures or tables and the context of the report by briefly explaining how they fit together (. . . "students' knowledge about prevention of heart disease improved during the program, as summarized in Figure 2"). As a general rule, tables are used to present detailed information that may be broken down into important categories, while figures are usually much less detailed and are used to illustrate how categories of information are related. For example, if we were evaluating a stop-smoking program, it might make sense to break our results down into categories describing the sex of clients and their smoking behaviors when they entered the program (heavy, moderate and light, for example). We could then produce a table or figure showing the success of the males and females in the program in terms of the "severity" of their habit.

As you can see in Figure 11-1, it is easy to see the relationship among the mean scores. Even though the numbers shown in the table report all of the same information that is in the figure, the impact on the reader is less dramatic, and determining the relationship among the categories of smoking behavior requires more imagination.

Scales

It is easy to manipulate the impression made by figures by choosing scales or illustrations that distort the results. Figure 11-2 shows how the change from a pretest to posttest can be made to look very different if the "right" scale is used.

Which graph in Figure 11-2 is correct? It depends on what you want the figure to show the reader. Another manipulation of scale is shown in Figure 11-3.

If you look carefully at Figure 11-3, you'll notice that the scale on the x-axis (the abscissa) changes in the middle. The change in scale makes

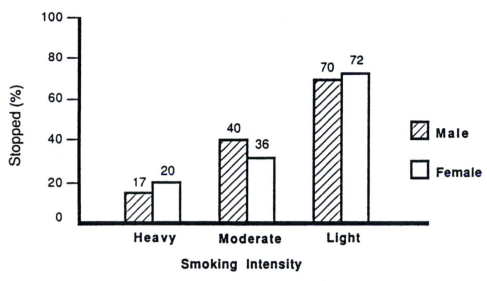

Figure 11-1. Smokers stopping (%) by sex and smoking intensity, N = 100, County Health Stop-Smoking Program, 1989.

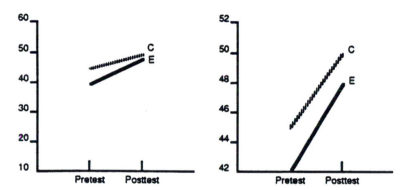

Figure 11-2. Mean pretest and posttest scores for experimental (E) and control (C) subjects, N = 100, County Health Program. Changing the scale changes the slope and the visual impression of the data.

interpretation of the graph impossible. Why did the scale need to be changed? Are the data from the first four periods for one or two years, and, if so, why is the graph drawn to suppress the fact that the number of uncollected bills increased so much after 1976? Keeping the scale constant might be embarrassing, but it is honest.

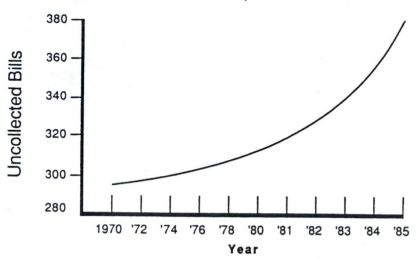

Figure 11-3. Number of uncollected bills by year. County Medical Center, 1985. Changing the scale in the middle of the graph confused the picture presented by the data.

Simplicity

Figures and tables are used to summarize information and make interpretation of the results of evaluation easier. When the tables and figures don't help to make the evaluation clear, then they are of little or no value. Simple tables and figures, those that make a clear statement, are usually the most helpful to the reader.

Writing reports for evaluations is really an exercise in communication. The most important features of good reports are that they are written with the needs and skills of the audience in mind, and the results are reported clearly and accurately. Since most audiences want the results summarized to some degree, finding the best way to "compact" the data is an important task. Tables and figures can be used effectively to present results in a "compact" way, but they must be well-designed and properly labeled.

READINGS

Morris, L.L., and Fitz-Gibbon, C.T.: *How to Present an Evaluation Report.* Beverly Hills, Sage, 1978.

Tukey, J.W.: *Exploratory Data Analysis.* Reading, MA, Addison-Wesley, 1977.

Wainer, H.: How to display data badly. *American Statistician, 38*(2), 137–147, 1984.

Wainer, H., and Thissen, D.: Graphical data analysis. *Annual Review of Psychology, 32:* 191–241, 1981.

GLOSSARY

The definitions to the terms listed here are provided to help you with the concepts presented in this book. In some cases, terms are defined expressly for the purposes of evaluation, and the same term will be defined somewhat differently in other sources.

ATTITUDE — Attitudes are essentially opinions that people have about various issues. Some believe that attitudes may predict behavior, hence their interest in measuring them. Others believe that attitudes reflect behaviors and think that behaviors instead of attitudes should be measured. For purposes of program evaluation, attitudes are the opinions of individuals or groups that have bearing on the program.

ATTRITION — When evaluations are carried out using designs that involve collecting information from people on more than one occasion, it's likely that you won't be able to find all the people every time you collect data. Such loss of subjects from the evaluation is termed "lost to follow-up" or attrition, as well as certain blue words. When attrition is high or when it occurs more in one group than another, the results of the evaluation may be affected.

BEHAVIOR — As used in this book, behaviors are observable actions of individuals or groups that can be counted or measured. For the purposes of program evaluation, behaviors are the actions of patients and/or providers that are related to the program.

BIAS — Evaluations are conducted to give us an estimate of the "true" effect(s) of the program. When the estimate differs from the "true" value, the difference is called "bias." The importance of bias isn't in its occurrence though, but in the effect it may have on the evaluation. If bias occurs because of our errors due to poor measurement techniques, a poor choice of evaluation design, etc., then it may be impossible to determine the effect of the program.

CONCURRENT VALIDITY — Validation of an instrument that is based on its ability to produce results which agree with results of other measurements carried out on the same individuals at the same point in time.

CONSTRUCT — An idea or theme that describes an intangible quality usually conveyed by a key word or phrase. Loneliness, for example, is a word that conveys a theme that identifies behaviors and situations that we define as signs of being lonely.

CONTROL — Establishment of a standard that defines what is "expected." A control group, for example, establishes what we would expect to occur in an individual or group if the program had not been carried out.

CONFOUNDING VARIABLE — Factors that compete with the program as an explanation for the results of an evaluation. If we were evaluating a program that teaches about colon and rectal cancer and the program participants had also read about colon cancer in another source (the experience of ex-president Reagan, for example), then we would not be able to determine whether the participants learned because of what they were taught or if they had learned from their reading, or both.

DEPENDENT VARIABLE — The measures used to evaluate the impact of the program on the individual or group. The dependent variables measure the impact of the independent variables. The dependent variable for a weight-loss program might be how much weight the people lose, or maybe their knowledge of proper eating practices.

EQUAL INTERVAL SCALE — A type of scale where attitudes are assumed to lie on a continuum from extremely positive to extremely negative. The scale is developed using statements to represent the continuum of attitudes in equally spaced gradations.

EVALUATION (program evaluation) — Evaluation is the comparison of a standard of expectations with the products produced by a program. Formative evaluation is focused on development of programs; summative evaluation is focused on assessment of the accomplishments of a program.

EVALUATION DESIGN — The strategy for collecting data that will make it possible to compare the program with a standard. Principles of experimental design are the bases for evaluation design.

EXPERIMENTAL DESIGN — Strategy for producing data to test hypotheses. Also known as "research design."

EXTERNAL VALIDITY — External validity refers to the extent to which the results of an evaluation might apply to other situations or, in other words, the generalizability of the results. A program with high external validity would be expected to produce the same results in many different settings. With low external validity, it's unlikely that the program would produce the same results unless carried out on the same people using the same procedures.

FACE VALIDITY—An instrument is said to have face validity if it appears to be valid. Properly used, this type of judgment is based on defensible criteria for measurement. This type of validity is not usually sufficient to establish validity of an instrument, however.

FOIL—The foils are the possible responses to a multiple-choice type item.

FORMATIVE EVALUATION—Evaluation that is focused on producing data that will help in the development of a program.

HYPOTHESIS—An educated guess about the relationship between two or more factors. A null hypothesis (a hypothesis of "no difference") is a statement made for statistical purposes and is the opposite of what is really believed to be true. A declarative hypothesis is a statement of what IS believed to be true.

INDEPENDENT VARIABLE—The factor or factors that are introduced or manipulated by a program or experiment. When a new program is introduced, the program itself is an independent variable. It is independent in the sense that it can be changed. We expect the independent variable to produce changes that can be measured using dependent variables.

INDEX—A way of expressing the relationship between two or more separate measures. Indices are commonly developed by combining measures mathematically.

INTERNAL VALIDITY—Program evaluation is said to have internal validity if the results measured at evaluation were indeed produced by the program activities. A program with high internal validity would be one where the intervention reliably produced the desired effects. A program with low internal validity needs to be revised or discontinued because it is not producing the desired results. A program must have internal validity to have external validity.

INTERVAL SCALE—A scale of measurement where the distance between values is known. Interval scales are continuous, and the values can be manipulated using nearly all mathematical operations.

KNOWLEDGE — For the purposes of evaluation, knowledge is cognitive, factual information that is related to the program being evaluated.

LIKERT SCALE — One of several possible methods for assessing attitudes. This method presents statements and the individual indicates his/her attitude by indicating their reaction from "strongly agree" to "strongly disagree."

NOMINAL SCALE — A scale of measurement where the object measured is named or classified. The values of measurement are only labels, so mathematical operations make no sense. Naming the sexes "female" and "male" is an example of nominal scale measurement.

OBJECTIVE — A statement that defines the expectations of a program. Properly developed, objectives identify what is to be done, the action that will be necessary and how the effects of the action will be assessed.

ORDINAL SCALE — A scale of measurement where the object measured is ranked in terms of order. The order may be defined as frequency of occurrence, size (large, larger or largest), etc. There is no implication of distance between ranks; only the rank of an object in terms of other objects.

PARALLEL FORMS — A system for determining the reliability of an instrument. Two equivalent forms of an instrument are developed, administered to the same individuals and the results compared. The two forms must be similar enough to measure the same thing, but sufficiently different to avoid predictable responses from the individuals taking them.

PILOT TEST — A pilot test is a pretest of an instrument being developed. Pilot testing is important to be able to revise the instrument to increase the efficiency of administration and correct any problems with language or organization.

PREDICTIVE VALIDITY — Validation of an instrument that is based on its ability to produce results that agree with other measurements carried out in the future on the same individuals. Entrance examinations, for example, may demonstrate predictive validity if they are able to identify students that perform well in training programs.

QUALITATIVE EVALUATION — Evaluation that compares performance with standards (see **Evaluation**) based on data that describe rather than measure. The roots of qualitative evaluation are in the social and behavioral sciences. Qualitative evaluation seeks to understand why programs produce results.

QUANTITATIVE EVALUATION — Evaluation that compares performance with standards based on data that are obtained by measurement. The roots of quantitative evaluation are in natural science. In essence, quantitative evaluation seeks to be able to predict (future) program results.

QUASI-EXPERIMENTAL DESIGN — Evaluation design where the requirements of experimental design cannot be fully accomplished.

RANDOM — A process is random when occurrence of events is not determined by any known rules.

RATIO SCALE — A scale of measurement where the values have all the properties of interval scale measurement and there exists a meaningful value of zero.

REACTIVITY — A process where individuals alter their behavior as a consequence of measurement. Keeping a daily log of cigarette smoking, for example, may induce an individual to decrease or increase smoking.

RELIABILITY — A reliable instrument measures consistently from person to person and setting to setting.

RESPONSE MODE — The method used to elicit answers to the questions asked in tests and scales. Commonly used response modes include true-false, multiple choice, completion, matching, short answer and essay.

SAMPLING — Sampling is the process of selecting objects or individuals for inclusion in an evaluation. Correctly executed, sampling is carried out to minimize bias in making selections. Common methods include simple random sampling, stratified sampling, cluster sampling and systematic sampling.

SCALE — A series of separate pieces of information that are put together to provide a summary measure or description. A series of items asking about various aspects of attitudes toward cancer may be put together to produce a "cancer attitude" scale.

SEMANTIC DIFFERENTIAL — A specific technique used to determine attitudes. The individual's attitude is inferred from the extent to which they agree and disagree with adjectives that describe reactions to the subject being studied.

SENSITIVITY — The extent to which an instrument is able to collect the specific information needed. A scale designed to measure self-confidence in a general sense would not necessarily be sensitive enough to produce good data from adolescents.

SPLIT HALVES RELIABILITY — Reliability that is established by dividing responses to an instrument into two groups and correlating the results obtained for each group. For most instruments it makes the best sense to form the groups by placing all even-numbered items in one group, and the odds in the other. The Spearman-Brown Prophesy Formula can then be used to correct the correlation coefficient for the total number of items in the instrument.

SUMMATIVE EVALUATION — Evaluation that is designed to assess program accomplishments. Summative evaluation is not focused on helping to develop an effective program as in the case of formative evaluation; rather, it is focused on evaluation of a program that is in operation.

SUMMATED RATINGS — A type of scale where the total score is the sum of results obtained from individual items. Scores from Likert scales are examples of summated ratings.

TEST-RETEST RELIABILITY — Reliability that is demonstrated by administering the same test or scale to the same individuals twice. The results from the two administrations are correlated to express the reliability.

TREND ANALYSIS — A type of evaluation design that is based on observing change over an extended period. The independent variable (program) is seen as having an impact if the trend changes.

USABILITY — A characteristic of instrument that addresses the issues of administration and scoring, clarity of language and any other characteristics that facilitate use.

VALIDITY — The extent to which a program produces results as intended or the extent to which an instrument measures as intended.

INDEX